© 1999 Algrove Publishing Limited

ALL RIGHTS RESERVED.
No part of this book may be reproduced in any form, inclu
permission in writing from the publishers, except by a reviewer who may quote brief
passages in a magazine or newspaper or on radio or television.

Algrove Publishing Limited
36 Mill Street, P.O. Box 1238
Almonte, Ontario, Canada K0A 1A0

Telephone: (613) 256-0350
Fax: (613) 256-0360
Email: sales@algrove.com
www.algrove.com

Library and Archives Canada Cataloguing in Publication

Lee, R. S. (Robert Stanley), 1932-
     All the knots you need : an illustrated guide / by R.S. Lee.

Includes index.
ISBN 978-0-921335-47-4 (bound).-ISBN 978-1-897030-03-5 (pbk.)

     1. Knots and splices. I. Title.

VM533.L42 1999   623.88'82   C99-901144-8

Printed in Canada
#18-10-14

About the Author

Bob Lee was raised on a homestead in northern Saskatchewan, living in a log house in an era when the only source of pocket money for children was from hunting, trapping, and digging seneca root. He went to a one-room country school and later to a one-room high school, graduating to become a teacher after a further winter of what was then called "Normal School". As well as teaching for a number of years, at various times he also worked as a farm hand, a prospector, a framing carpenter, a pipe fitter, and a roofer before serving 6 years as a navigator in the RCAF and later graduating (*cum laude*) with an engineering degree from the University of Saskatchewan. This range of experience, plus his longtime hobby of fly fishing, gave him both reason and opportunity to use a wide variety of practical knots in diverse vocations, all of which led to the writing of this book.

All The Knots You Need

An Illustrated Guide

by R. S. Lee

Table of Contents

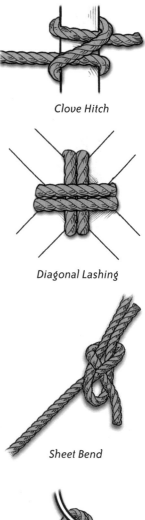

Clove Hitch

Diagonal Lashing

Sheet Bend

Anchor Bend

Double Sheet Bend

Painter Hitch

Taut-Line Hitch

Monkey's Fist

Chinese Button Knot

Reef Knot

Heaving Knot

Triple Bowline

Introduction

Anyone who has seen *The Ashley Book of Knots* may well ask why anyone would produce another knot book, for Ashley, in describing nearly 4000 knots, has said it all. I asked myself that question. My answer is that Ashley strove for completeness, with many knots that are beautiful, but difficult to tie, and quite impractical for someone who simply wants to do a job in as simple a way as possible. This book presents far fewer knots, but in a more useful format, showing what knots are suited to a given task and showing how to tie them so that one who is not a master rigger will be able to produce them with ease.

The same knot may have many names, according to the trade or the part of the country in which it's used. The sheet bend and the weaver's knot are identical, but the sailor and the weaver tie them in different fashions for different purposes, and in very different materials. If you see one that I call the grapplechoker, and you've known it all your life as the whipfitter's bend, I make no apologies, but I'd certainly like to hear from you about it. Even the definition of what constitutes a knot can differ. To a sailor, a knot appears only at the end of a rope. If a sailor is attaching a rope to an object, he uses a hitch. If attaching two or more ropes to each other, he uses a bend.

All knots are here illustrated as though tied by a right-handed person. This may make tying them a bit more difficult for left-handers, but as most lefties have adjusted to the difficulties of a right-handed world, I'm sure they'll have no problem in working out the differences. Where the description refers to rope with a twist, rather than braided rope, it's generally assumed that the rope has a right-hand or Z lay, which means that the slot between strands has the same alignment as the center line of the letter Z. Left-hand lay is called the S lay.

The components of a rope, from larger to smaller, are the strands, the yarns and the fibers. The lay will usually alternate, i.e., for a Z laid rope, the strands will be S laid and the yarns Z laid.

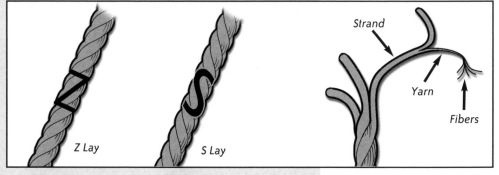

Figure 1 - Lay and Components of Rope

A few terms are necessary before we can describe how to tie a knot. The working end of the line is called, not surprisingly, the end. The rest is the standing part. A bight is an open loop (see glossary). Loops may be overhand, with the end over the standing part, or underhand, with the end under the standing part.

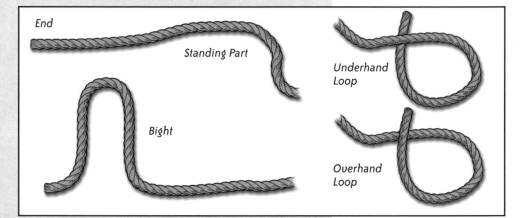

Figure 2 - Rope Terminology

Knowledge of eight or ten knots is all most of us should ever need for daily activities, but that knowledge must include how to use them and why one is more secure than another or easier to undo in an emergency. This book will cover those points. It will also generally define the materials used for practical knotting, the relative merits of the natural and synthetic fibers, and reasons why some fibers are better for a particular task than others. It is less hazardous to acquire this knowledge through reading than through bitter experience.

Choosing the Right Material

With the great selection of fibers now available, choosing the right rope or cord is not as simple as in the days when manila, sisal and cotton made selection easy. On high performance sailing vessels, for example, the choices involving size, strength and weight make for an infinite number of compromises. You have to decide what qualities are most important and select the fiber that provides the best compromise. Here are the main factors to consider.

Price

Nylon is more expensive than polyester, which is higher in price than polypropylene. Manila and sisal are becoming harder to find, and accordingly may cost more than their relative value can justify. The newer materials, such as the aramids, HMDPE (high molecular density polyethylene) and Vectran®, exhibit all the fine qualities one needs in rope and cord, but their cost may be prohibitive.

Stretch

Stretch is one of the factors that's both good and bad. It makes for excellent shock absorption; you can jerk a nylon tow rope without vehicle damage. However, if you're a tightrope walker, you'll be happier with aramid rope and guy lines that have little give.

Strength

Strength and size should be considered simultaneously. For many applications, the weaker fibers are more than adequate. For example, if the rope's strength is to match that of a man hauling on it, a breaking strength of a few hundred pounds is enough. Most fibers achieve 500 pounds breaking strength in 3/16" diameter, and nearly all do so in 1/4". That's much too thin for comfortable hauling barehanded. Therefore what may be needed (in the working rigging of a sailing dinghy, for example) is more bulk rather than more strength.

Contact with water can affect the strength of a rope. Nylon loses as much as 15%, whereas manila and cotton gain strength by 15% or so. Polyester, polypropylene and polyethylene are unaffected, as their fibers don't absorb water.

Weight

For something like a water-ski tow rope, you need a rope that floats, so it's easily retrieved and stays out of the propeller. Polypropylene or polyester are good choices. If weight matters, remember that most synthetic fibers absorb little water, most natural fibers absorb a lot.

Hand

The old term "hand" refers to how a rope feels. If you're working without gloves, the rougher natural fibers can be hard on your hands. The slipperiness of some of the synthetic fibers can be a nuisance, and whether the rope is stiff or flexible is worth considering for some applications. A calf roper's lariat, for example, is almost too stiff to knot, but holds a loop well.

UV and Chemical Resistance

Will the rope be out in the sun? Some fibers, polypropylene for example, can be pretty well destroyed by a year of sunlight. Manufacturers usually add protective pigment to materials with low resistance to ultra-violet light before the fibers are produced. Another solution, used in braided rope, is to cover the non-resistant core with a UV-resistant material.

Where oil, gasoline or chemicals will come into contact with the rope, polyester is a better choice than nylon or manila. Nylon is weakened by acids, Dacron® by alkalis. Polypropylene, cheaper and weaker, resists both.

Type of Construction

Laid rope (twisted) is traditional and still the best for many applications, where splicing is needed, for example. The down side is that it can be more stretchy than braided rope, less flexible and harder on the hands. It also displays more pre-formed tendencies when coming from the reel or coil.

Braided rope offers a manufacturer great scope in compensating for drawbacks, in some cases using combinations of several fibers to create a rope with the desired characteristics. A weaker but UV-resistant braided cover can be made to protect a strong core that would be destroyed by direct sunlight. Where rope has adequate strength, but must be thicker for easier handling, a bulky core may be included, made up of weaker and cheaper filler fibers. For special purposes, there are ropes with an outer layer for wear resistance, a bundled (unbraided) fiber middle layer and a wire core.

Ability to hold its shape may determine the type of construction. A rope used with blocks should be resistant to deformation. It should stay round in cross-section under pressure, so it tracks well and isn't damaged internally. Frequent flexing or shape change causes internal friction between the fibers and can greatly reduce strength in a rope that looks perfect on the surface.

Reaction to Heat

Fibers with a low melting point, for example, polypropylene, can be a bad choice for applications where there's a lot of friction resulting in heat.

Other Factors

The long list of factors to consider includes conductivity. Rope for tree work near power lines, for example, requires a fiber with high electrical resistance, so conductivity is near zero.

Rope running over pulleys, especially where the flex direction changes, must be able to take flexing without destruction of internal fibers. Here's where stretchy nylon works well, even though it deforms.

Knot Strength

Another consideration is knot strength. Some fibers lose a lot of strength when knotted, requiring splicing instead; others are less affected. Knot strength also depends on the choice of knot. When ropes break, they generally do so just at the exit from the knot, apparently a function of deformation and sharpness of bend. In recent tests of strength carried out by Bridon Fibres using a number of natural and synthetic fibers, and tests done at the College of Agriculture of the University of Minnesota around 1920, the breaking strength of common knots is as shown in the following table.

Knot	Percent of Straight Breaking Strength
Eye Splice	100
Short Splice	96
Long Splice	92
Timber Hitch	78
Carrick Bend	77
Round Turn and Half Hitches	73
Clove Hitch	70
Fisherman's Bend	70
Bowline	60
Sheet Bend	55
Overhand Knot	50
Square (Reef)	48
Figure Eight	46
Sheepshank	46

There is no solid general agreement on the relative knot strengths given above. One respected writer, for example, assigns only 55% to the carrick bend.

Resistance to Rot and Abrasion

Most synthetic fibers are resistant to rot. Where it's impractical to dry lines completely before storage, natural fibers are a bad choice. Resistance to abrasive wear can be important. The slick-surfaced line may be hard to grip, but perfect for use where there's abrasion.

Whipping

Cut rope ends tend to unravel and become an untidy mess of disorganized strands and yarns. Whipping prevents that, giving a neat appearance and making the rope easier to knot or reeve through an eye. For many artificial fibers (polypropylene, nylon, polystyrene, etc.) a simple way to stabilize the ends is to heat treat them. A flame will do, but as application of a flame tends to cause ends to mushroom, it should be avoided.

Whipping is the application of a winding made of a cord of much smaller diameter. In the days of hemp and manila rope, waxed linen thread was the usual material. It's still available from some suppliers, but if you can't find it, use what's available, such as braided fishing line.

Start by laying the end of the whipping cord along the rope, then wind the cord over itself, beginning about one and a half diameters from where the whipping is to end. If the rope's end is badly frayed, this end point should be at the beginning of sound rope. About a half diameter from the

For temporary control of loose ends when splicing, a narrow wrap of duct tape is quick and effective.

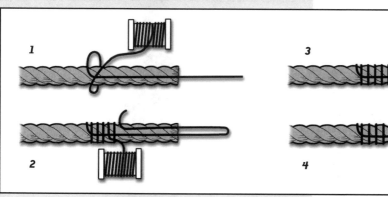

Figure 3 - Whipping: *wraps must touch each other (see cover photograph).*

finish, you make provision to tuck the end under at the completion of the winding. There are two usual ways to do this. The simplest is to reverse the loose end of the cord, laying it alongside of the rope with the end far enough back to provide a good grip after you have wound over it. Then continue to wind the cord tightly for several more turns. Put the end of the winding cord through the loop. Grasp the end of the part forming the loop and draw the other cord end back under the winding. Trim the ends closely and tuck the stubs between the windings for neatness.

Coiling

If you are coiling a rope that is fixed to an object at one end, start coiling at that end. It will help avoid the kinks that develop when there's no end free to twist as you coil. To hang up a coil, when you reach the last turn or so, form a loop and pass it around behind the coil near the top, then through the center of the coil above the wrap. The loop can then be on a peg.

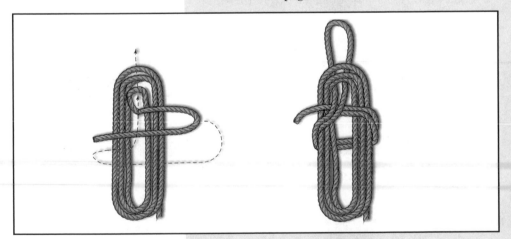

Figure 4 - Preparing a coil for hanging.

Bag Knot

A knot that is little used now, but is highly useful if you need to hold an article under tension while tying, is the bag knot. I remember it from closing grain and potato sacks on the farm. When the bag is so full that you can barely draw it closed, this knot will still allow you to secure it. Unlike the miller's knot, traditionally used for this purpose, a simple tug spills it.

Firmly grip the bag top in your left hand, so that the material is under tension from the pressure of the contents. Slip the cord between the little finger and ring finger of your left hand, leaving at least a two-inch end exposed. Wrap tightly once clockwise under your left hand. On completion of the wrap, bring it up under the little and ring finger, over middle and forefinger and wrap tightly again, keeping the cord above but in close contact with the previous wrap until just before bringing the end up. When the second wrap is done, bring the end up between your forefinger and middle finger behind the cord that previously passed over them, then tighten the resulting knot.

Although this is a simple friction knot, it holds well even with rough usage. The truly great merits of it are that it is a knot you can tie with one hand while maintaining control of the object with the other, and it can be spilled quickly by pulling up on either exposed cord end.

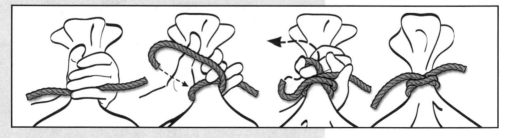

Figure 5 - Bag Knot

Bowline

A sailor tells me that in these days of shrouds, stays and halyards made of wire or steel cable, he could now get by with no more than six knots in various combinations. One of the most necessary would be the bowline, as it has so many uses. It's one of the simpler knots to tie, perhaps best described using the method taught to Boy Scouts for generations. Take the end in the right hand, standing part (the "tree") in the left. Throw an overhand loop in the standing part (this forms the "rabbit hole"). Bring the end up through the loop ("the rabbit comes out of the hole") around the standing part ("around the tree") and back down through the loop ("the rabbit goes back down the hole"). The only tricky part is to draw up the knot so that the loop formed is firm and the size you want it to be. You will sometimes see it tied with the end toward the outside of the loop rather than inside as shown, but that's not the traditional way, and has led to sharp words by scoutmasters.

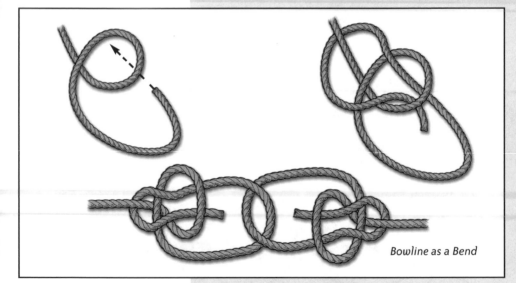

Bowline as a Bend

Figure 6 - Bowline

Sailors, mountain climbers and steeplejacks will tie a bowline in a safety line around their waists, cowhands will make an emergency lariat with the standing part through a bowline at the end, and the bowline makes a good hitch to throw over a post or tie to a ring. When used as a safety line knot, it's a good idea to throw a half hitch in the end as a stopper knot. Two bowlines can also be used as a bend, to tie two lines together to make a longer line. It's not as neat as a sheet bend, but it's easy to untie and won't slip.

One-Handed Bowline

Old sailors tell of tying a bowline one-handed while up in the rigging in the teeth of a gale. It can be a useful skill if you need a safety rope with one hand already engaged. Assuming that one end of your rope is attached above you, and you're maintaining your safety grip with your left hand, loop the other end round your waist. Holding the end in your right hand, cross your wrist over the standing part, then down and bring it up next to your body to form a loop around your wrist. The tricky part then begins; your hand is through the "hole" and it must pass the end round the "tree", releasing the end and grasping it again to pull it back down through the "hole". Practice helps.

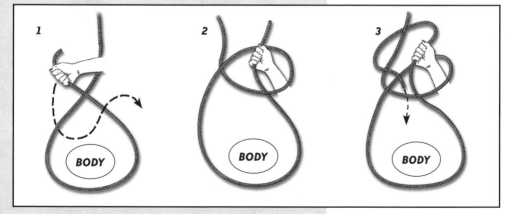

Figure 7 - One-Handed Bowline

Bowline in the Bight

Sometimes it's necessary to tie a bowline in the middle of a line. This is known as a "bowline in the bight". Form a bight in the line, loop it to make the "hole", then push the middle of the bight up through the hole and pass it back down around the whole arrangement, then up and tighten to form the knot.

A bowline in the bight is good for hoisting a person, with either one leg in each loop, or with legs in one loop, the other loop around the back for support. It's also used to tie up a boat. The bight is slipped over a post or bollard with the ends attached to the boat fore and aft.

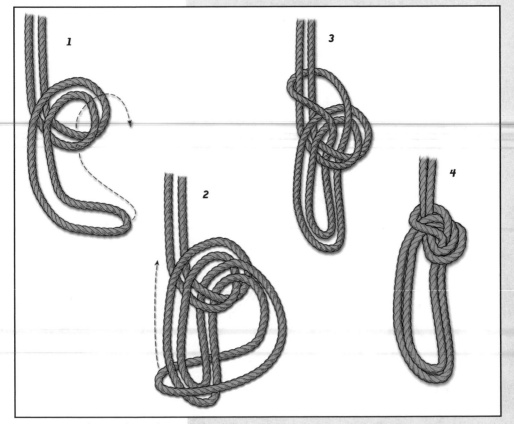

Figure 8 - Bowline in the Bight

Triple Bowline

A version of the standard bowline, but tied in the middle of a line, gives three loops, which can be useful if a person is to be suspended. The three loops can provide more support, one loop being under the armpits, one to sit in, and one just behind the knees. The tricky part of this knot is the adjustment of the loops to the appropriate sizes, an exercise in patience.

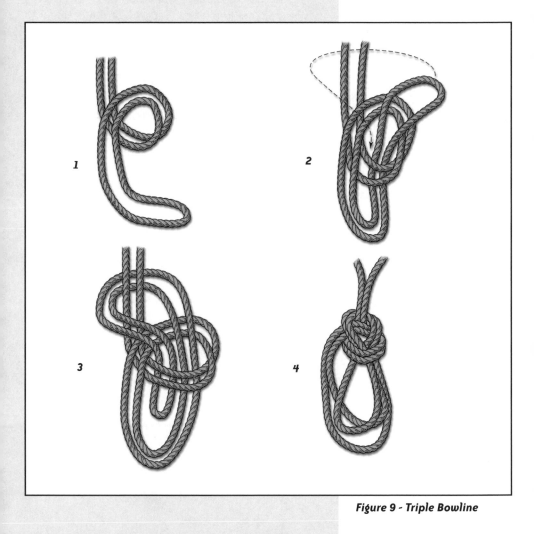

Figure 9 - Triple Bowline

17

Spanish Bowline

The Spanish bowline is also known as the Chair Knot, as it's used by firefighters and mountain rescue teams to hoist or lower people. It's also used to hoist objects such as ladders or stretchers in a horizontal position, with loops of equal size slipped over the ends. When used in rescue, one end goes under the person's armpits, the other behind the knees. Loops can readily be enlarged by drawing down more of the standing part. The relative sizes of the loops can then be changed by enlarging one loop at the expense of the other. When the overall size and relative sizes are set in this way, drawing the knot up firmly will hold the loops as they are set. Sizing is very important for hoisting an unconscious person, to avoid any chance of slipping through the loops and falling. For additional safety, take the end around the standing part in a half hitch. Another way to use this knot to hoist a person is to put one leg through each loop, with a half hitch in the standing part under the armpits.

To tie, the steps are:
1. Make a bight with crossed ends as shown in Figure 10, Step 1.
2. Pull the parts through the bight to form the position shown in Figure 10, Step 2.
3. Give the resulting bights a half twist as shown in Figure 10, Step 3.
4. Reach down through the bights and pull up the sides of the lower loop to form the two main loops, A and B.
5. Tighten the knot, using more or less of the standing part as necessary to make A and B the desired size.
6. For insurance, a half hitch of the end around the standing part after adjustment will add security, but it should not be necessary if the knot is carefully tightened.

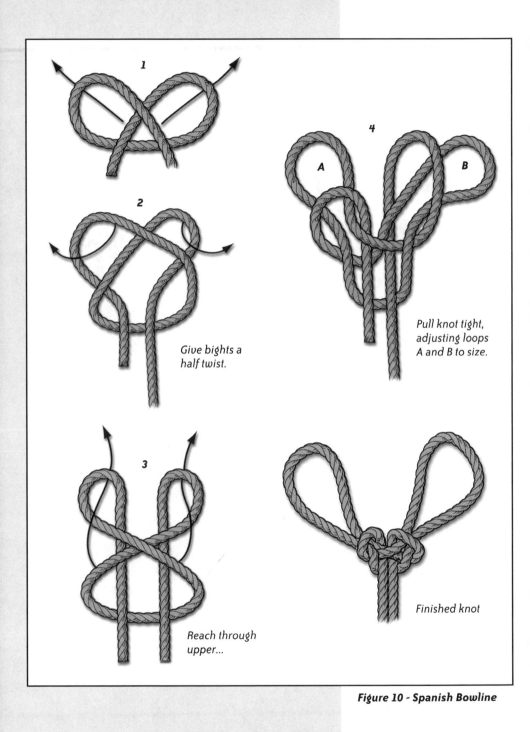

1

2

Give bights a
half twist.

3

Reach through
upper...

4

A   **B**

Pull knot tight,
adjusting loops
A and B to size.

Finished knot

Figure 10 - Spanish Bowline

French Bowline *(Portuguese Bowline)*

The French bowline, like the Spanish bowline, is used for hoisting an unconscious person, but it is easier to adjust, as the loops are related; reduce one, enlarge the other.

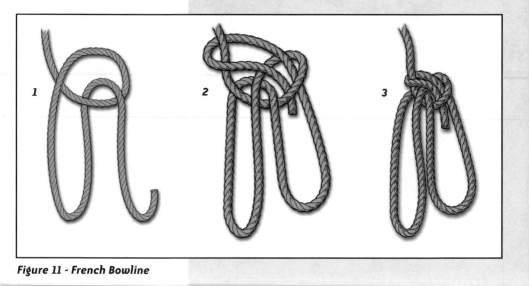

Figure 11 - French Bowline

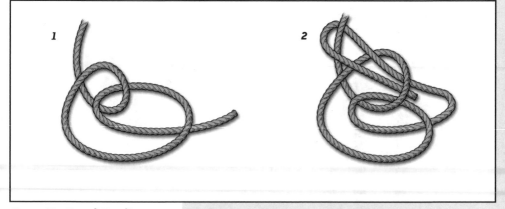

Figure 12 - French Bowline
(Another Way)

Lightning Bowline

A lightning-fast way to tie a bowline depends on a quick bit of preparation. As you approach the post or bollard around which you intend to tie it, you must make a quick overhand slip knot in the standing part. Flip the end around the post, through the slip knot, and yank the standing part. The slip knot spills and a bowline results. It takes practice, but amazes an onlooker who sees it for the first time.

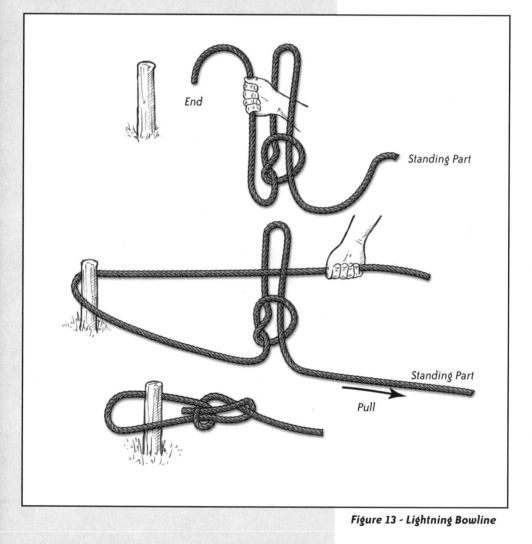

Figure 13 - Lightning Bowline

21

Half Hitch and Marline Hitch

The Half Hitch is so simple that it can scarcely be called a knot, but it forms a part of many other knots. It is, in effect, the start of an overhand knot around an object such as a post, spar or rope. If an actual overhand knot is tied round the object, it is a Marline Hitch, a better knot for security when a series is tied round a roll or package, as it tends to stay put better when tightened.

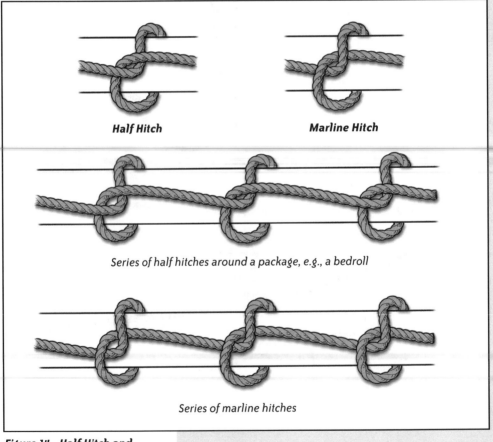

Half Hitch　　　　　*Marline Hitch*

Series of half hitches around a package, e.g., a bedroll

Series of marline hitches

Figure 14 - Half Hitch and Marline Hitch

One of its applications is in the round turn and two half hitches, used as a hitch for mooring a boat or tying a horse to a ring, post or bollard. Take a round turn around the anchoring object, followed by two half hitches around the standing part. Be sure that the two half hitches form a clove hitch round the standing part, rather than a lark's head.

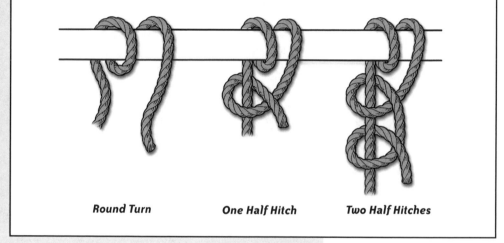

Round Turn   **One Half Hitch**   **Two Half Hitches**

Figure 15 - Round Turn and Two Half Hitches

Lark's Head *(Ring Hitch)*

Lark's head is not a name used by the old sailors, even though they used the knot. They'd have more likely called it a ring hitch. The name came into the literature through an early English book on knots that used a French book as a source, translating *tête d'alouette*. The knot is handy for attaching identification tags to luggage, placing an adjustable ring in the bridle of a kite and any similar use where equal force is applied to each of the ends. To tie it on a ring, the simplest way is to pass a bight through the ring, then pass the ring through the bight.

Figure 16 - Lark's Head on a Ring

An important use of the knot by horsemen is an exception to the equal force rule, but as it's tied in a leather strap, the knot holds anyway. In this case, it's the standard cinch knot, holding the cinch tight to keep the saddle in place.

Figure 17 - Lark's Head as a Cinch Knot

Clove Hitch

The clove hitch is a simple knot with many uses, both by itself and in combination with other knots. For example, it's present in the round turn and two half hitches, as the two half hitches form a clove hitch. It's easy to tie, especially when it can be slipped over a post.

The easiest way to tie it is to form two overhand loops. Lay the first over the second and the clove hitch is formed, ready to slip over a post or bollard. It's a bit more complex if it must be tied around an object. In that case, pass the end around the object twice, the first time over the standing part. The second time round, slip it under the standing part.

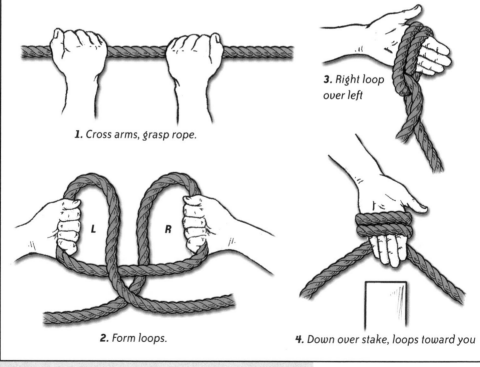

1. Cross arms, grasp rope.

2. Form loops.

3. Right loop over left

4. Down over stake, loops toward you

Figure 18 - Clove Hitch

If you have to tie a long rope to a series of posts or stanchions to enclose an area (crowd control, for example), you can tie it in the middle of a length of rope in a couple of quick motions as shown in Figure 18. Cross your arms, right over left, grasp the rope, then twist your hands in opposite directions as you uncross them. You'll be holding two loops; lay the right over the left and drop the resulting clove hitch over the post. Snug up the line to eliminate sag and move on to the next.

The nautical uses of this knot are endless, so we won't attempt to cover them. One point to note is that it's best where there is tension on each of the parts. If only one end is under tension, the clove hitch can slip. If you're using it in that situation, secure the free end with a half hitch or two around the standing part.

Buntline Hitch

The buntline hitch is almost exclusively a sailor's knot, having been used in the days of sail to attach a sheet or halyard to a shackle, but it could be useful to others. Its main advantages are that it takes up little space, and it can stand plenty of shaking without coming loose, as when attached to the grommet of a flag snapping in the wind. To tie it, run the end through the grommet or ring, then back and make a clove hitch around the standing part.

Figure 19 - Buntline Hitch

Taut-Line Hitch

A useful knot employed by arborists in trees is the taut-line hitch. It is simple to tie and, where the ropes are of slick material and the hitch rope is about the same size as the vertical rope, it locks better than the Prusik knot. Two of them can be used for climbing, just as a Prusik is used. More often, it is used as a movable pivot point for suspended work.

Assuming you have a vertical rope through your work area, and you want to set a pivot point from which to suspend a harness, take a short piece (six feet or so) of rope of the same, or preferably smaller, diameter than the vertical rope and attach it to your harness. With the other end tie the taut-line hitch round the vertical rope to enable you to move about with it as support. Of course, you should have a safety line as backup in case the hitch slips.

The hitch consists of two wraps round the vertical rope, followed by a clove hitch above the wraps.

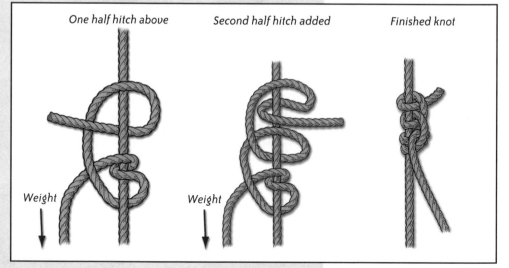

One half hitch above   Second half hitch added   Finished knot

Weight   Weight

Figure 20 - Taut-Line Hitch

Hoisting Hitches

There's a whole class of knots used for hoisting awkward items such as barrels, logs, sheets of plywood and bundles of shingles.

Timber Hitch

As its name indicates, the timber hitch is used for dragging or hoisting timber, logs or planks. Its main merit is its ease of tying and untying, but it's a temporary knot, not highly secure. Pass the end of the rope around the load near one end, around the standing part, then several times around the other part of the bight.

Figure 21 - Timber Hitch

Killick Hitch

For better control and security, it's wise to make one or more half hitches toward the other end of the load, which makes it into a Killick Hitch. That keeps the load in line with the direction of lift or pull, and guards against the danger of the timber hitch loosening, as the rope in its vicinity is not worked while the load is dragged or hoisted.

Figure 22 - Killick Hitch

Barrel Hitch *(Jug Hitch)*

To hoist a pail, barrel (or jug), the barrel hitch is a good choice. It's simple to tie and maintains the load in an upright position, essential if you're hoisting an open container partly filled with liquid.

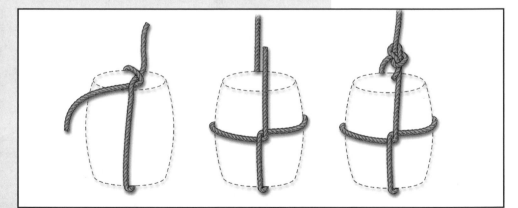

Figure 23 - Barrel Hitch

Place the load over the rope and tie an overhand knot loosely over the top. Open the overhand knot and slip half down around either side of the load. Tie the ends of the hoisting rope together above the load. If you're working with just one end of the hoisting rope, tie a bowline to secure the end to the standing part.

For an enclosed barrel-shaped load such as an oil drum, a dunnage bag or a short log, bend the ends of a piece of rope together, lay the load across the resulting loop, then slip one bight of the loop through the other and lift with the bight.

If the load must be kept horizontal, spread the supporting bights and lash each to the end of the load nearest it.

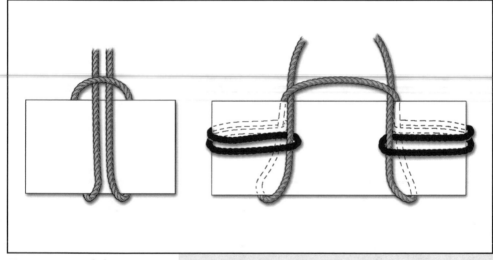

Figure 24 - Barrel Sling

Often the hoisting gear will terminate in a hook. The classic way to attach a rope to a hook is the cat's paw.

Cat's Paw

Form a bight, then fold it over the standing part to make two loops. After twisting the loops in opposite directions three or four times, slip them over the hook. The resulting arrangement will take the weight without slipping, but can be easily loosened again.

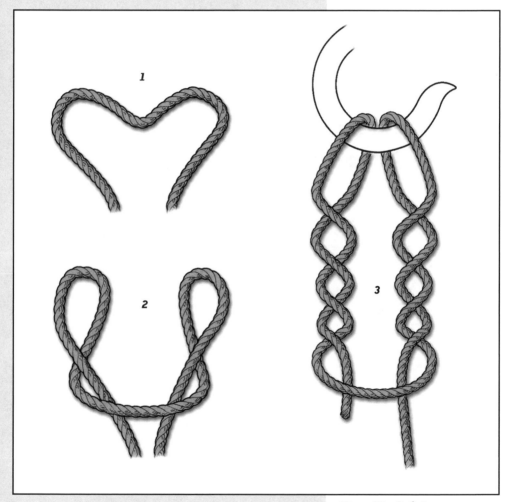

Figure 25 - Cat's Paw

Quick Hitch

Another hitch for the same purpose is not as well known, but effective. Form two bights in the rope as though preparing to tie a sheepshank, with the long end to the right. Grasp the resulting three lines in the middle with the left hand and wrap the right-hand end several times round them. Take the two bights, one in each hand, and slip them over the hook. The right-hand end takes the weight. The hitch will not slip, but falls apart when taken off the hook.

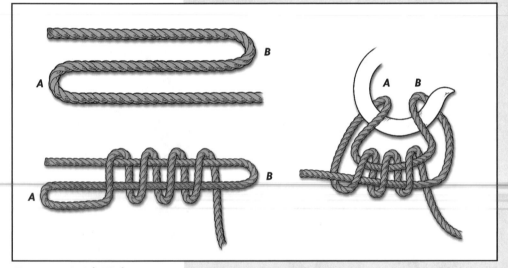

Figure 26 - Quick Hitch

Figure 27 - Blackwall Hitch

Blackwall Hitch

The blackwall hitch must be the simplest rope arrangement that can be called a knot. It's fast and, if tension is maintained, it doesn't slip. All the same, don't trust it where danger or damage would be the result of it letting go. To tie it, make a loop in the line, slip it up over the hook, then down into position and apply tension. It works best when the line is large enough to fill the gap in the hook.

Scaffold Hitch

It's often useful to rig up a short plank as a scaffold for sitting on while painting or carrying out repairs. The rope round the plank should be readily adjustable, but shouldn't allow the plank to rotate in use. This scaffold can do the job.

Wrap the line round the plank twice. With the ends hanging down, you'll have three parts lying on top of the plank. Transfer the one nearest the center of the plank to the middle position. Then take the one that's nearest the center (formerly the middle one) and pass it over the end of the plank. Pick up the two ends and tie a bowline. The standing part then is attached to the anchor point. Repeat for the other end of the plank.

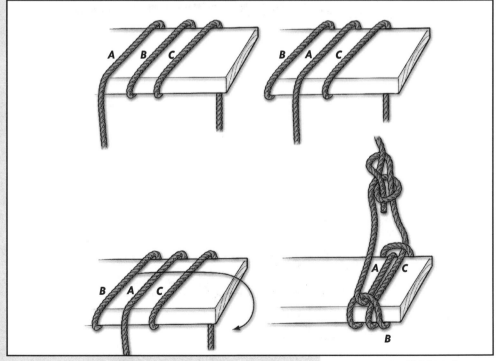

Figure 28 - Scaffold Hitch

Fishing Knots

The fly fisher for trout needs five basic knots. From the reel spool out, they are: backing to reel, backing to fly line, fly line to leader butt, leader butt to tippet, tippet to fly.

Backing to Reel

The knot attaching the backing to the reel is simply two overhand knots. Pass the backing around the spool, then with the end, tie an overhand knot around the standing part, followed by another one in the end as a stopper knot.

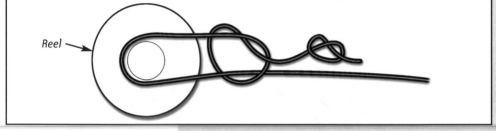

Figure 29 - Backing to Reel

Backing to Fly Line

The Albright knot is a standard backing-to-line attachment. Form a bight in the fly line, lay the end of the backing along the fly line with a foot or so overlap, then wrap the backing around itself and the bight toward the loop of the bight. Finally slip the backing end through the fly line loop and carefully draw all tight, making sure the backing lies in neat adjacent turns.

Figure 30 - Backing to a Fly Line

Fly Line to Leader

There are at least three knots commonly used for this junction, differing mainly in difficulty of tying, but also slightly in bulk and neatness. They are the nail knot (and nailless nail knot, same knot but different method), the needle knot and the multiple-turns overhand knot.

- **Nail Knot**

  Lay a short section of fine hollow tubing (one is usually supplied with a fly line, or the pump needle for inflating soccer balls will do, if the end is filed off) along the fly line tip. Hold line, leader and tube parallel, with 6 or 8 inches of leader overlapping the line. Then wind the leader over itself, the line and the tube for 4 to 6 turns. Poke the butt of the leader back through the tube, then withdraw the tube to leave the leader end inside the wrap. Keeping the turns pressed between the fingers, tighten the turns by pulling alternately on the leader's butt and standing part. When the turns are evenly spaced and closely clasping the line, pull both ends of the leader to strongly tighten the knot. Trim the end.

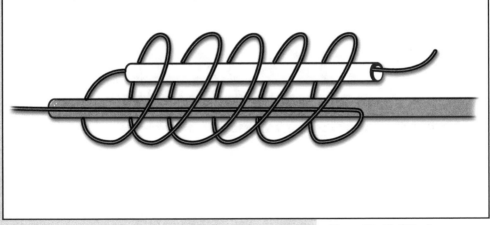

Figure 31 - Nail Knot

• Needle Knot

The needle knot is the neatest of the line-to-leader knots, but is difficult to tie on small lines, lighter than #6. Start by cutting the end of the leader butt at a slant, so that it terminates in a sharp point.

Figure 32 - Cutting end of leader

Thrust a needle into the center of the end of the fly line, so it emerges a quarter inch or so from the tip. Withdraw the needle and run the leader butt into the channel made by the needle, pulling it out of the hole in the side far enough to make a nail knot. If the threading operation proves too difficult because the leader is too thick, try putting the fine tip of the leader in from the other direction and drawing it out from the line end. Then proceed to tie a nail knot, drawing the knot up just at the point where the leader emerged from the line. This makes a secure knot with the line and leader in perfect alignment.

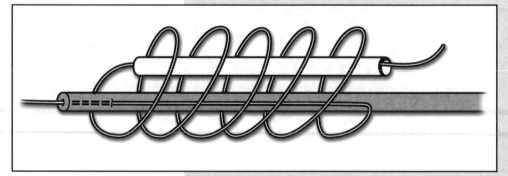

Figure 31 - Needle Knot

• Nailless Needle Knot

If you must tie a leader to your line and haven't a nail or tube handy, it can be done. Run the leader into the line as before, but wrap it four or five times around the line somewhat above where the finished knot is to be. Bring the end back and lay it alongside of the line, pointing away from the line end.

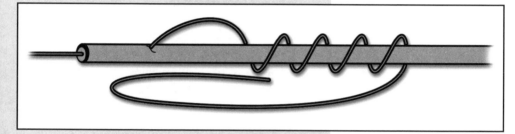

Figure 34 - Nailless Needle Knot (Step 1)

Now begin to unwind the wrappings from above the knot location, so that the leader wraps over its end.

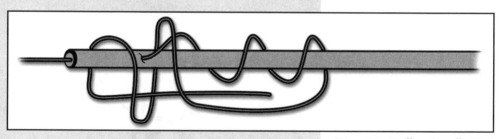

Figure 35 - Nailless Needle Knot (Step 2)

With care, you can transfer all the wraps so they cover the leader end. Draw all tight, holding the tip of the leader and drawing the rest of the leader back out of the line end, while keeping the turns neatly parallel as they tighten up.

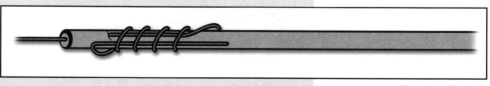

Figure 36 - Nailless Needle Knot (Step 3)

Of course, this procedure will work without piercing the end of the line, but simply laying the leader alongside the line as you begin, as will be necessary if you have a light line and a heavy leader butt.

Fishermen who use a variety of leaders, e.g., a long fine leader for dry fly fishing and a short heavy one for streamer use, can set up an easy way of changing leaders without tying new knots each time. It's done by tying a perfection loop in the leader butt and the leader to be changed. They can then be readily linked and unlinked at the loops.

• **Perfection Loop**
Form an underhand loop, grasping it between thumb and forefinger. Bring the end up around the thumb to form a second loop. Then lay the end in between the loops and draw the second loop over it and down through the first loop. Tighten to form a single loop about 3/4" in diameter. The leader and line may then be joined as shown.

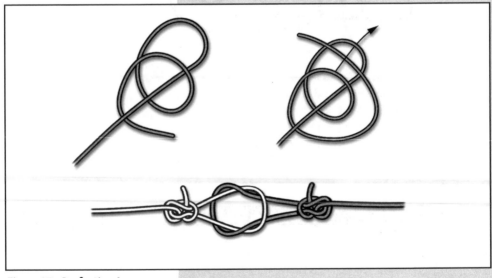

Figure 37 - Perfection Loop

• Multiple Overhand Knot

All of the previous knots do a good job, but are a bit fiddly to tie. A simpler method, but one that results in a thicker knot, is much more easily tied. Overlap the fly line and leader by a foot or so, then tie an overhand knot. Carry both parts through the resulting loop two or three more turns. When this knot is tightened up, it has the same degree of security as the other, but a bit more bulk. Tighten both elements equally and carefully. Adjust the turns in a neat parallel arrangement, to make the result look good.

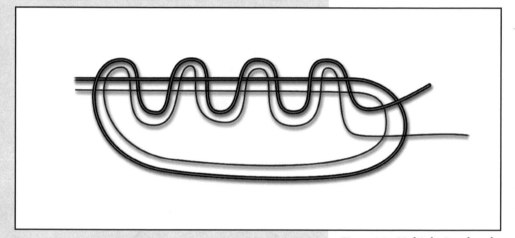

Figure 38 - Multiple Overhand Knot

Leader to Tippet

The Blood or Barrel Knot is the standard for joining two lengths of monofilament of similar diameter. Cross the pieces, overlapping by 8 inches or so. Hold the crossing point between thumb and forefinger. With the other hand, make five turns of the leader round the tippet, then insert it between the pieces at the other side of the crossing point. Change hands, keeping control of the parts placed so far by pinching them, then make five turns of the tippet round the leader. Insert the tippet end into the same opening as the leader end, but in the opposite direction. Hold the ends and pull the standing parts to draw the knot up tight. This is really a four-hands operation, but it can be done by two with practice.

Figure 39 - Leader to Tippet

Tippet to Fly

The Clinch Knot is most commonly used, with a variation, the Improved Clinch Knot. Thread the tippet through the eye of the hook, then wind five turns around the standing part. Put the end through the loop created at the eye. If you tighten it up at this point, you have the clinch knot. If you carry the end back through the bigger loop before tightening, the improved clinch knot results.

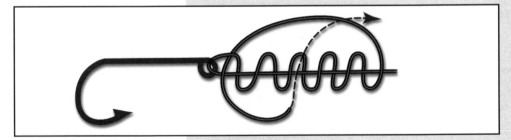

Figure 40 - Tippet to Fly

Knot Lubrication

A popular belief about knots in monofilament is that one should always wet them with saliva before drawing them up tight. Supposedly this reduces friction, allowing the knot to draw tighter. With less friction, there is also less heat, which is believed to weaken the monofilament.

Stopper Knots

Cut ends of rope tend to come undone, especially the stiff polypropylene or polystyrene ropes. A stopper knot is a temporary fix. (For a proper fix, the ends should be whipped.) The name comes from its other use as a means of stopping a rope from slipping through a ring or the hand of someone hauling on it.

Figure 41 - Overhand

Overhand

The simplest stopper knot is an overhand knot, not pretty or secure, but fast.

Figure-Eight

The figure-eight knot is the next step up. It looks better and is less likely to slip off the end.

Noose Knot

By itself a noose knot would be a poor stopper, as a tug on the standing part would spill it. To make it into one of the better stoppers, with more bulk to prevent slipping through a ring, make a loop in the end and grip it in the closed noose. A quick tug on the end will spill it, another advantage of a good stopper.

Figure 42 - Figure-Eight

Figure 43 - Noose Knot Stopper

41

Ashley's Stopper

A stopper knot originated by Ashley is similar to the above. It consists of a noose knot with the end gripped in the closed noose. Less easy to spill than the knot described above, it has a neater look to it.

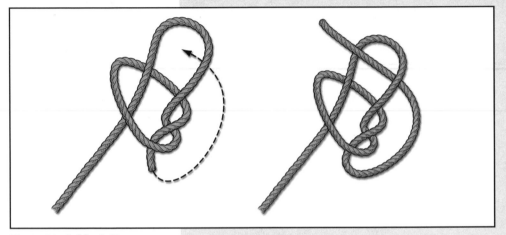

Figure 44 - Ashley's Stopper

Figure 45 - Crown Knot

Crown Knot

The crown knot forms the beginning of the back splice (see below). Tie it by unlaying several inches of rope, then form a bight in one strand. Form a bight in the second strand with the end passed over the first strand. Form a bight in the third strand over the end of the second and stick the end down through the bight in the first.

Back Splice

The back splice is not a splice in the general meaning of the word, to join pieces of rope, but it is formed in much the same way as the short splice. It is a means of finishing a rope end to prevent fraying and unravelling. It also thickens it, so that it can be used to prevent the rope slipping through the hand, a hole or a block. This allows it to be used to make chest or bucket handles.

To tie it, unlay several inches of rope and tie a crown knot. Draw it tight and shape it carefully so that it appears symmetrical when viewed from the end of the rope. Then pass each strand in turn over the first strand next to it and under the second, crossing against the lay. Continue tucking strands in this way at least twice. For neatness, you can trim away half of each strand's yarns before you carry out each of the subsequent tucks, continuing until you run out of strands or patience.

Wall Knot

The wall knot is similar to the crown knot; the difference is that the ends come up instead of down. It is seldom used on its own, but it forms the base of an interesting knot, the Matthew Walker. Unlay six or more inches of rope. Apply a whip finish (or bind with an elastic band or a strip of duct tape) below the unlaid portion. Working in the direction of the lay, pass each strand up through a bight in the following strand. Draw tight and lay up the unlaid portion.

Figure 46 - Back Splice

If you wish to continue and tie a Matthew Walker, do not draw the strands tight.

Figure 47 - Wall Knot

Matthew Walker

Although the Matthew Walker knot's use is limited today, it was a highly important knot aboard sailing ships. We include it partly because it has an interesting history. Clifford Ashley tells of a sailor named Matthew Walker, sentenced to death by a judge who had been a sailor himself. The judge offered a pardon if the sailor could tie a knot that the judge could neither tie nor untie. The sailor (in private) unlaid half of several fathoms of rope, tied a Matthew Walker knot, relaid the rope neatly and offered it to the baffled judge for his release.

The Matthew Walker knot is said to be the only one named for its inventor. The Hunter's Bend, popularized by Dr. Hunter, is considered to have been invented earlier by a man named Smith, and Dr Prusik's knot, truly the Prusik hitch, is apparently not accepted by reason of the sailor's definition of a knot, i.e., something tied in the end of a line.

One use aboard ship was in forming beckets for the handles of wooden buckets. Today craftsmen find it of value for chest handles. It acts as a stopper knot to prevent rope from being pulled through a hole.

To tie it, start with a wall knot. Pass each strand up through the next bight in sequence one more time. Draw all strands tight, lay up the remaining unlaid portion and apply a whip finish.

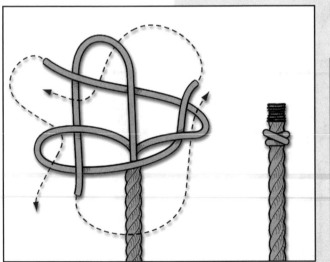

Figure 48 - Matthew Walker

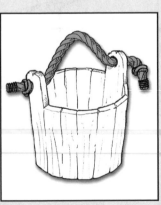

Figure 49 - Matthew Walker as a stopper on bucket handle

Chinese Button Knot

The Chinese button knot is unlikely to be used as a stopper knot; stopper knots usually need to be tied in a hurry, and the button knot needs time, care and attention to get it right. However, it looks good when it's done, and can be used as a button when tied in fine cord. The story goes that it was the traditional button on Chinese garments, wearing at the same rate as the garment, and never breaking as bone or ivory buttons might. It's a bit bulky to go through a buttonhole, so a loop of cord usually accompanies it to hold the garment closed.

The sequence in tying it is to form a loop, then a second loop over the first with the end passing under the standing part. After that it's simply over, under, over, under and then work the knot into shape.

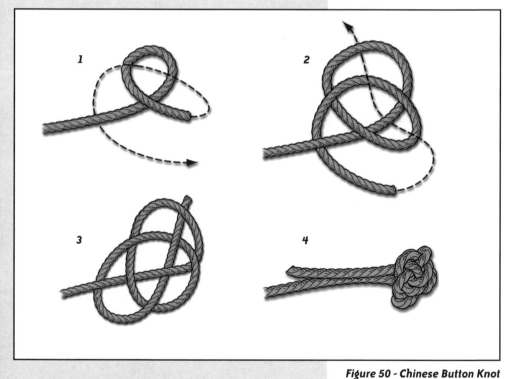

Figure 50 - Chinese Button Knot

Tie-Down Knots

One of the main uses of knots these days is to tie down loads, whether on a pack horse, on top of a van or in a truck box. The diamond hitch has all the virtues of a good tie-down knot; it is easy to tie, easy to tighten, and easy to remove. However, for a simple, quick restraint, whether to hold a rope over a load, to stretch a clothesline, or to attach tent to tent peg, the simple tie-down is a good start.

You may have read in older Western stories of the tenderfoot faced with loading a pack horse and expected to secure the load with a diamond hitch. To most, the diamond hitch was an impenetrable mystery, even when shown its tying and use. The so-called double diamond hitch could be complex, especially when tied on the back of a fractious mule with a tendency to lash out at anything passing behind.

The single diamond hitch is simple to tie and still useful. There was a good reason for using the diamond hitch, in addition to its security. As the pack horse moved, the load settled and shifted, so that after a while the tie-down system began to work loose. The diamond hitch could be easily tightened; loosen a couple of half hitches, reef on the line, replace the half hitches and all was well for a few more miles.

Simple Tie-Down

Make a butterfly loop in the standing part above the point of attachment. Carry the end through the ring, or around the tent peg or clothesline pole, back through the butterfly loop and haul tight. For a permanent knot, a series of half hitches will hold all firmly. If the knot is soon to be easily released, take the end around the standing part and bring a loop back through between the two parts (a slipped half hitch). A tug on the end will easily release it, yet it will hold while under tension. If there is likely to be any slackening of tension, a slipped noose or a round turn and two half hitches will be more secure and should not jam.

Diamond Hitch

There are many ways to tie the diamond hitch. Some of the variations lie in the method of attaching the line to the tie-down points, depending on whether they are posts, loops, rings or pack saddle corners. We'll assume you have a pickup truck box containing a load covered with a tarp, and six attachment points. If your set-up differs, modify accordingly.

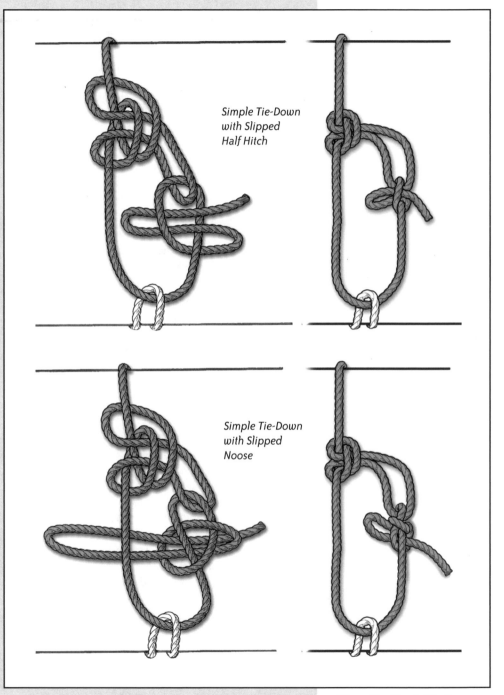

Simple Tie-Down
with Slipped
Half Hitch

Simple Tie-Down
with Slipped
Noose

Figure 51 - Simple Tie-Down

Attach your line to the center point of one side. Use a lark's head, if the attachment point is a ring, a clove hitch if it's a post. Pass it across and back rather loosely, then take the line around the starting point (if it's a ring, simply pass it through). Grasp the center of the resulting loop and give it three or four twists. Carry the line on to one of the adjacent corner tie-downs. Here's where it's best if the tie-down is a post or ring that the line can simply pass around or though, for ease of tightening later. Now pass the line back to the center, through the twisted part and back to the next corner tie-down. Carry on back to the center, through the twist, to the next corner, back to the center and finally to the last corner. Haul on the line to tighten, adjusting in the center as necessary, then attach the line with a clove hitch or round turn and half hitches. (Some packers will proceed back to the center and to the starting point for final attachment, but this can cause clutter there and is unnecessary.) Work your way around the corners, tightening once again. After travelling a short distance, stop and loosen the final attachment and haul all tight once more. This operation should be done periodically, until there is no discernible loosening.

When the diamond hitch is tied on a pack saddle, instead of passing from side to side, the twisted center portion aligns with the back bone of the animal. The corner loops may be attached to rings in fore and aft cinches, or the line may be passed under panniers on either side of the horse, or any number of other set-ups may be used. In any case, loading a pack horse and securing the load is beyond the scope of this book. It's an art and a skill that is ingrained in the life style of the old packers.

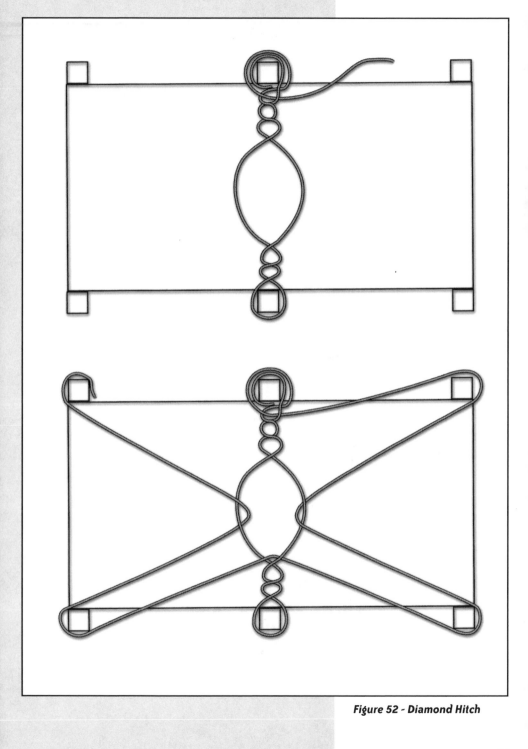

Figure 52 - Diamond Hitch

Knots for Throwing

Sailors used a variety of knots for heaving line from the vessel to the dock or between ships. The intent of the knot was to create sufficient weight at the end that the heaved end would carry the rest of the line with it. Some consisted simply of a ball of the line's material knotted in the end; others, of a more permanent nature, had a weight confined in the end knot. Two of the simpler ones are given below.

Heaving Knot

Sometimes called an end-weight knot or a heaving-line knot, it resembles a tightened hangman's knot.

Form two bights to make an S in the line. Pass the end through the first bight, then once around the first bight. It's critical to make this first wrap around only the first bight. You may see it tied with the first wrap around both, but that can allow

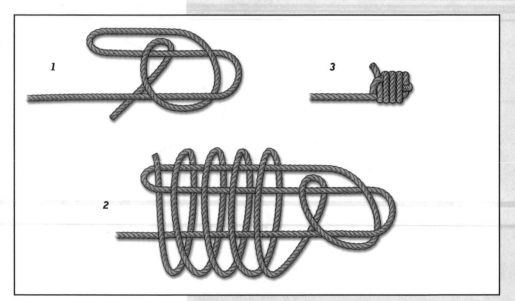

Figure 53 - Heaving Knot

the knot to unwrap and come apart. Follow up by wrapping several turns around both bights, finishing by passing the end through the second bight. Tighten by drawing up the first bight, then standing part. This knot can be tied round a rod-shaped weight, if the extra weight is needed.

Monkey's Fist

The monkey's fist is easy to tie badly but it's somewhat more difficult to tie neatly than the simple heaving knot, especially in a high friction material such as manila, that takes much work to draw it up tightly so it looks uniform. One of its advantages is that it can be tied around an object such as a wooden ball, if it is to float (as when a line was flung to a man overboard), or around a lead or iron weight to fling over a tree branch or from one vessel to another.

It may be tied with either two turns or three turns. The illustration shows two for simplicity. Start by taking two turns of the line, leaving a fair space in the middle of the loops. Continue by taking two turns round the first loops at right angles to them. Then take two turns outside and at right angles to the second set, but inside the first set. At this point, add the ball, if you wish, then work the knot tight. Tying the end into the standing part with a bowline adds security and neatness. For a truly professional appearance, use three turns. Bring the end alongside the standing part and splice them together as you would an eye splice.

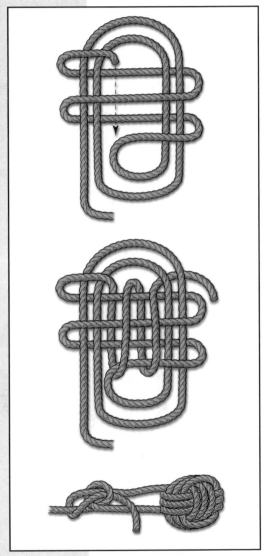

Figure 54 - Monkey's Fist

Painter Hitch
(Highwayman's Hitch)

The secondary name for this knot, the highwayman's hitch, comes from the old word for the man who robbed travellers, the highwayman. The highwayman supposedly had to untie his horse in a hurry to make his getaway. You may have seen this knot in old Western movies. As the bad guys raced from the bank they had just robbed, a quick tug on the dangling line freed the horse for the flying mount and dusty gallop out of town.

The painter hitch is so-called because it's a natural to use in attaching a boat's painter to a bollard, as it holds well, but releases instantly. We show how to tie it to a hitching rail. Note that as the loops come free, no part of the line is left looped around the rail, so it simply falls loose.

Another possible use, when plenty of rope is available, is to allow a climber to tie it with a long end, come down with the aid of the standing part, then yank the end to retrieve the rope on reaching the bottom. The obvious danger is inadvertently putting weight on the wrong strand part way down. It's not recommended.

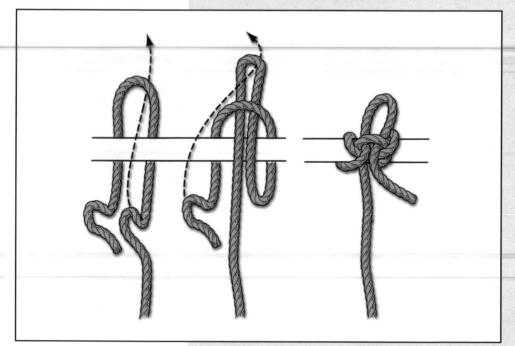

Figure 55 - Painter Hitch

Prusik Hitch

The Prusik Hitch is a favorite of rock climbers, spelunkers and arborists, who use it to ascend a fixed rope. Its value lies in the fact that it slides easily along a thicker rope until tension is applied, when it locks firmly. It should always be tied in cord that's much thinner (say, one-third the diameter) than the rope it slides on, and preferably in a non-stretching material (e.g., Dacron®, not nylon).

The Prusik hitch gets its name from Carl Prusik, the inventor. According to Geoffrey Budworth, Prusik invented it during WWI to mend broken instrument strings.

Usually two loops are used. The first loop should be just long enough to fit under your foot when the knot is at eye level. The second knot should be at waist level. The knots are slid up the rope alternately. The climber's weight is in one, locking it; then the other is slid up for the next step. It works, but if the rope is icy, the cord wet, etc., don't trust your life to it. (An alternative, especially when the ropes are slick material and of similar size, is to use the taut-line hitch.)

To tie it, form a loop in the thinner material, pass it round the thicker rope and through itself; then repeat and tighten. For slippery materials, three loops may be of help.

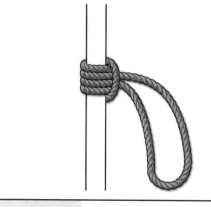

Figure 56 - Prusik Hitch

Reef Knot *(Square Knot)*

Undoubtedly the best-known knot in the world is the granny knot. The knot used by most of the world to tie shoelaces and parcels is a reef (or granny) knot with the ends not pulled through, but formed into loops. A granny knot is inefficient and you should always use a reef knot in preference to it. If this book does nothing else for you but stop you from tying granny knots, it will have earned its price. The reef knot, also known as the square knot, is most useful in tying up packages (such as furling sails). It should not be used as a bend, because of its tendency to spill when an end is tugged, especially in stiff rope.

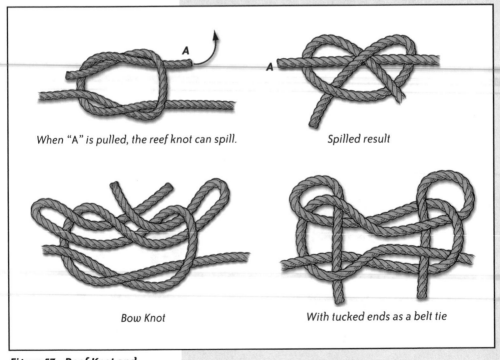

When "A" is pulled, the reef knot can spill.

Spilled result

Bow Knot

With tucked ends as a belt tie

Figure 57 - Reef Knot and Bow Knot

However, if you must use it as a bend, for example, to tie the ends of a cord belt together, you can add security by tucking the ends down behind the bights. It secures the knot and makes it look a bit decorative.

It has an interesting twin, the rogue's knot, rarely tied for legitimate purposes. The rogue's knot will slip a bit, and may even spill, when tension is applied, especially when tied in a stiff braided rope. Supposedly it was used to close a sailor's dunnage bag so that tampering could be detected. If a thief untied the knot, he'd likely retie it with a reef knot, tipping off the owner that someone had been into his belongings. Another use was by the escape artist's assistant, who would apply the knot as a restraint, invite the spectators to check its tightness, then marvel as the great man easily slipped free. There is an oft-quoted principle of knots that says no adjacent (touching) parts of a knot should have a tendency to move in the same direction when the knot is under tension. The proper reef knot meets this requirement, but in the rogue's knot adjacent parts move in the same direction, so the knot slips without friction.

Figure 58 - Rogue's Knot

Sheepshank

The sheepshank is a rope shortener. It's one that all old Boy Scouts know, but if you ask if they have ever used it, not one in twenty can say so in truth. However, if a rope has a frayed (weak) section, the sheepshank can be used to avoid cutting the rope. Tie it so that they frayed section is not strained.

One use that's sometimes attributed to it, but which entails both risk and wasted rope, is the Steeplejack's knot. Assume that the steeplejack is at the top of a flagpole, and must use his rope to slide down, but wants to release it at the bottom.

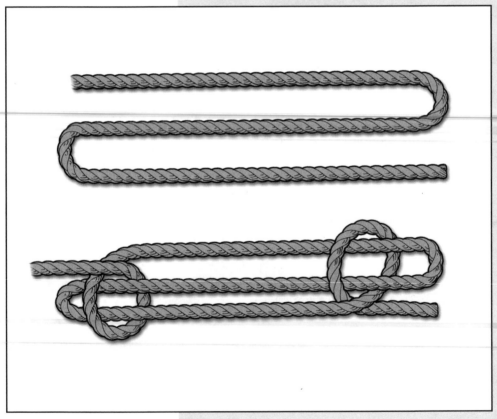

Figure 59 - Sheepshank

He can tie a short sheepshank at the top, then before he comes down, he cuts the middle line of the sheepshank, the one that passes through both half hitches. (That's the section that would contain the frayed part mentioned above.) The knot will hold if kept tight, he can give the rope a few shakes and down it comes (most of it). It's not recommended, especially if the rope is soft and flexible. There are better methods, ones that save both rope and life, such as the painter hitch.

Figure 60 - Steeplejack's Knot

Sheet Bend

The sheet bend is the simplest, most useful of the bends, especially good for tying together lines of different diameters. Its name comes from its use in fastening (bending) a sheet (rope used to control a sail) to the clew of a sail.

Slippery Sheet Bend

Figure 61 - Sheet Bend

Form a bight in line one, bring the end of line two up through it, around the standing part and then under itself across the bight. If the lines are stiff, a double sheet bend will be more likely to hold under released tension. It is tied by passing the end of line two around the bight on the first line twice before crossing under itself. If quick release is needed, the slippery sheet bend is a good choice. The difference is that a bight is passed under line two rather than just an end.

Flag Bend

Another name for this knot is the flag bend, because it's the ideal knot for tying the tags on flag corners to the flag rope, as rope and tags are usually different diameters.

Figure 62 - Double Sheet Bend

Weaver's Knot

Weavers use the identical knot to repair broken threads, but tie it in a different fashion.

Figure 63 - Weaver's Knot

Bookbinder's Knot

A similar knot, but tied with a needle, is also known as the bookbinder's knot. It's interesting by reason of the fact that it's tied with one end of one of the lines, but formed in the other end. One of its advantages is that it allows you to slide the knot along the fixed thread until it is flush with the mended material. It's handy when doing rough sewing, as it can be tied without releasing the grip on the needle.

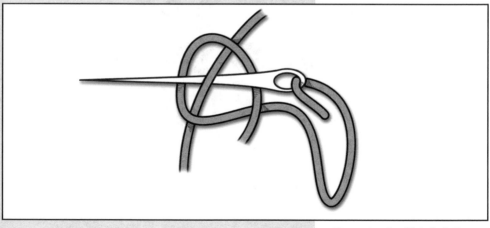

Figure 64 - Bookbinder's Knot

Figure 65 - Short-End Sheet Bend

Short-End Sheet Bend *(Shoelace Repair)*

One of life's little problems is the broken shoelace, especially when there isn't a new one available, there's not time enough to undo the whole thing and relace it after knotting, and the end exposed at the eyelet is too short to tie to. There's a method of tying a sheet bend when one end is very short that can save the day. Tie an overhand noose in the longer part, slip the short piece through the noose, then pull both ends of the longer piece. A sheet bend results, securing the short end.

Three-Way Sheet Bend

A three-way sheet bend can be useful where three lines come together under tension.

*Figure 66 - Three-Way
Sheet Bend*

Warning: *A fast method to tie the sheet bend, sometimes given in books on knots, is to hold a bight in line one with one hand, throw an underhand loop over it with the other, then put the loop end down through the bight and draw up firmly. This looks like a sheet bend, but the standing part is anchored under the end, the reverse of how it should be.* **Don't use it.** *Easing of tension can cause it to let go.*

Figure 67 - Fast Sheet Bend

The foregoing may seem like unnecessary repetition of the same knot, but that's the nature of knotting. For example, few rope workers are aware that the sheet bend and the bowline have the same structure; cut a bowline's loop and the two parts are joined by a sheet bend.

Figure 68 - Sheet Bend and Bowline

Carrick Bend

The carrick bend has not always been given the credit it deserves. As it is often used for decorative purposes, its significant value as a working knot is sometimes ignored. In truth, the carrick bend is the ideal knot for joining two thick tow ropes, or for any job requiring a heavy pull. It has two advantages: its breaking strength ranks it at the top of the list of bends; it does not jam. If a round stick or dowel is placed in the center of the knot before tension is applied, it may be untied without effort. Be warned, however, that the carrick bend may slip when tied in slick synthetic fiber rope. For those materials, it's necessary to seize the ends to

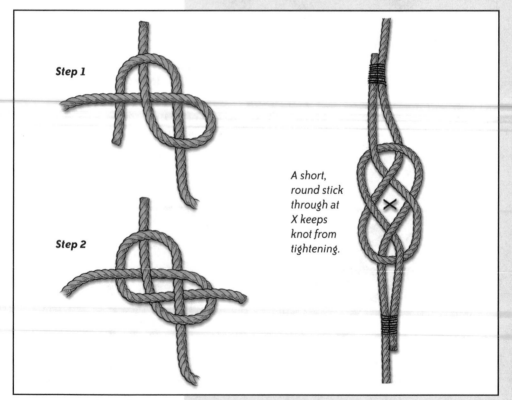

Step 1

Step 2

A short, round stick through at X keeps knot from tightening.

Figure 69 - Carrick Bend

the standing parts, or half hitch the ends once or twice. It's especially useful for very thick lines, but requires some care in forming the knot as the pull is applied. If the ends are not seized, there will be considerable initial slip as the knot forms into a shape more cubic that flat. You should experiment with it a few times before you need it.

Anchor Bend
(Fisherman's Bend)

Another hitch (in spite of being called a bend) useful for tying to a ring, spar or rail, is the anchor bend, so called because attaching a line to a small boat's anchor ring is its main use. This knot solves the two problems of tying to a ring: it's secure and it doesn't jam. It's a round turn through the ring, then a half hitch that passes through the round turn. Though that should do the trick, another half hitch around the standing part makes it secure.

Figure 70 - Anchor Bend

Hunter's Bend
(Zeppelin Bend)

Here's an interesting knot that is relatively new. One story of its invention is that it was used to moor airships, so it's sometimes called the Zeppelin bend. Though it's a good knot, especially for the new slippery materials, it's not as simple to tie as the blood knot or sheet bend, so that limits its use. It is basically two overhand knots intricately linked. To tie it, begin by laying the lines parallel (step 1), then form a loop (step 2). Pass the ends through the loop from opposite sides (step 3), ensuring that all crossings are as shown in the diagram. Then form the knot, shaping it carefully as you draw it tight. It may take some working to form it correctly.

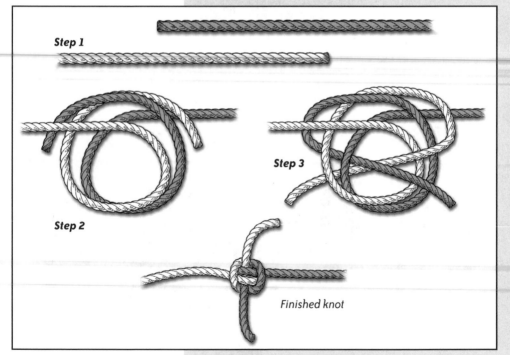

Step 1

Step 2

Step 3

Finished knot

Figure 71 - Hunter's Bend

Ashley's Bend
(The Stamp Knot)

Clifford W. Ashley's great book *The Ashley Book of Knots* (ABOK) has many admirers. Some of them have begun a campaign, still unsuccessful at this writing (but we wish them success) to have Ashley honored by a commemorative US Postal Service stamp. The proposed design pictures Ashley, one of his paintings and one of his original knots, ABOK #1452, which he did not name, but referred to merely as "Another original bend that…appears to be strong, secure and compact."

It's easy to tie, consisting of two linking loops, with the ends passing in the same direction through the common portion.

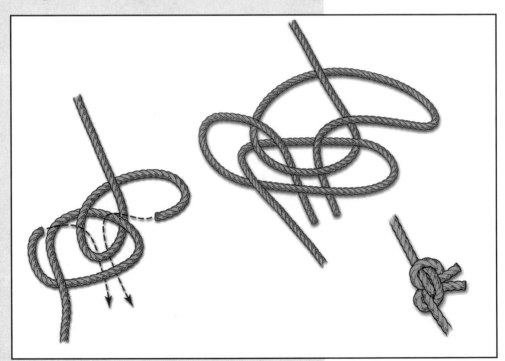

Figure 72 - Ashley's Bend

Strap Knots

There's a family of knots used formerly by farm workers for quick mends of harness straps. The simplest is the grass knot formed as shown here. When carefully drawn up, it lies flat with the ends emerging in the same direction. The grass knot may have been so named through its use by weavers of grass mats. Its second most common use among farmers was for joining wire ends. It holds well and can be tied without tools, even in very stiff wire.

Figure 73 - Grass Knot

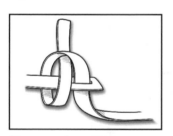

Figure 74 - Strap Knot

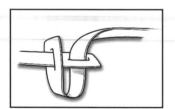

Figure 75 - Strap Knot

When the farm hand had a sharp pocket knife handy, he would have had more options for mending a broken leather line, such as the strap knot. A quick slit in the standing part, with the end of the free part brought through and half-hitched around the standing part made the knot adequate until rivets could be used for a more permanent mend.

A similar fix could be done by slitting both straps, slipping the slot of the free part over the standing part, then passing the free end through the slot in the standing part.

Splices

There's a lot less need for rope splicing than there used to be, especially with the advent of braided rope and the virtual disappearance of manila, but it's still a useful skill to have. The two main methods of joining two ropes are the short splice, which is the strongest, and the long splice, used when the rope's diameter must not be increased, as when it must go over a pulley. Two other splices are the eye splice, used to make a permanent loop in a rope end, often containing a thimble, and the back splice, a means of finishing the end of a rope.

Short Splice

The first step in starting a splice is to unlay each of the ropes for a sufficient way back to give enough working length. That unlaying creates the first problem – a lot of loose strands to keep track of. It's a good idea to slip a tight rubber band over each of the ropes before you begin. Then, as you work on one end of the splice, the strands at the other end can be tucked under the rubber band, where they will stay put and not fray or get in the way. If you're working with synthetic fibers, it helps to melt and wipe the ends of the individual strands before beginning.

We'll assume that the rope is three-strand, without a core. If a core is present, it's usually there for bulk, not strength, so cut it at the junction. If the rope is four-strand, proceed as for three-strand. Crotch the ends together so that each of the left end strands is between two of the right end strands. Then tuck one of the left strands over one of the right strands and under the next one, working against the lay. Repeat for each of the strands. Pull the junction up tight. The first set of tucks is finished. Repeat for at least one more tuck, and preferably two more, pulling all tight after each tuck. When the last tuck has been made, trim off the ends and roll the finished splice under your foot to work the strands together.

There's room for refinement of this process, such as tapering the strands at each tuck. By this means, and adding more tucks, the splice can be made almost invisible, except for a slight thickening at each side of the junction point.

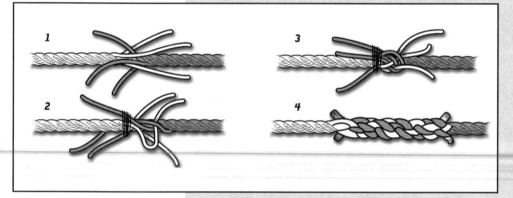

Figure 76 - Short Splice

Long Splice

The long splice has one advantage: it doesn't thicken the rope, so the splice can pass through a block and over a sheave or pulley. Its disadvantages are that it takes more rope, it's weaker, and it's not as easy to finish the terminations of the individual strands.

Start by unlaying a dozen turns or so of each rope and crotch them together. Unlay one strand a further five or six turns of the left rope and replace it with its equivalent strand from the right rope. Be sure to twist the replacement strand tightly as you lay it into place. Repeat, replacing a strand of the right rope with the equivalent strand from the left. You will then have three points on the combined rope with two strands emerging from it. At each of these points tie an overhand knot so the ends lie parallel. From here there are several ways to proceed, none perfect. Which you choose will depend on how neat you want the result to be and how much extra thickness is allowable.

- Tuck each strand over one and under one, halve the number of yarns and repeat. This thickens the rope a bit, but controls the loose ends.

- Trim yarns from the strands and tuck them in with the lay, that is, winding each around the other, continuing to trim yarns so as to taper the strands, until they merge with the rope.

- If the splice must be thin, cut off half the yarns in each strand, tie the overhand knot and dispose of the ends by one of the means described above, tapering further as you go.

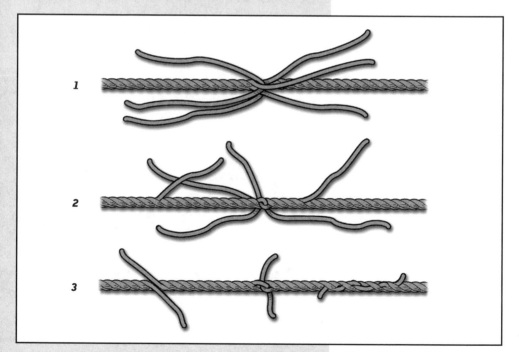

Figure 77 - Long Splice

This may not be easy with some stiff, wiry synthetic fibers. With these, a little judicious application of a propane torch at the end of the job can tidy up the splice.

Grommet

The grommet is included here because its construction is similar to that of the long splice. Grommets are used for handles, bumpers and even for the old game of ring toss. Decide on the circumference of the grommet, then unlay from (preferably) three-strand rope a piece somewhat longer than three times that circumference. You'll have material for three grommets. Form a circle of the size the grommet is to be and lay the rest of the rope carefully in with it, tightening the twist of the strands if need be, to ensure that the result is well laid. When you have gone around twice, there are several ways to handle the problem of how to lay in the ends. You can simply cut the strand off to butt against the first end, but that will probably require whipping to keep it from unlaying. It's better to choose one of the ways described above for handling the ends in a long splice.

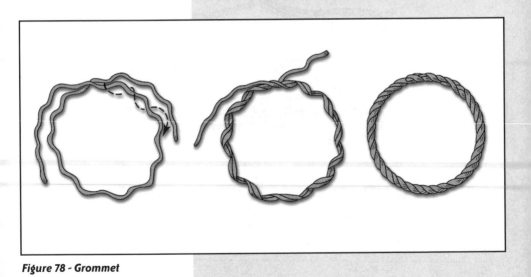

Figure 78 - Grommet

Eye Splice

The eye splice is made by laying the end of a rope back on itself and splicing it in to form a permanent loop. It is used to make a stiff rope into a lariat, or to enclose a thimble where the loop will be subject to wear. It may also be used to attach a ring. In that case, allow the portion that passes through the ring to remain unlaid into its constituent strands where it touches the ring.

Start by unlaying the rope for a few inches and seizing the standing part to keep it from unlaying further. Tuck the middle strand (B) under one strand of the standing part at right angles to it. Next take the inner strand (A) and tuck it under the next strand of the standing part, adjacent to the first. To tuck the third strand (C), it's easiest to turn the work over first, then tuck the strand under the remaining strand of the standing part. Tighten all up and if you are working it round a thimble, or intend to place a thimble in it later, check that the loop is the right size. Then proceed as before, tucking the strands in turn, over one strand of the standing part and under the next. Continue for at least three sets of tucks. Cut off the ends or taper them and tuck once more before cutting. Roll and work the splice to set the strands into position.

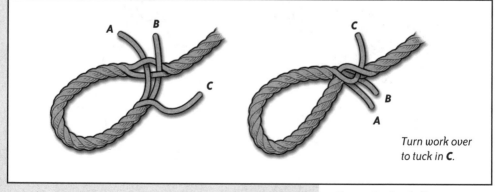

Turn work over to tuck in **C**.

Figure 79 - Eye Splice

Rope Work on the Farm

A successful farmer must be a bit of a carpenter, welder, electrician, mechanic and in some cases a veterinarian. It's an advantage if a sailor's knowledge of knots is added. Most of the knots needed by the farmer have been mentioned above, but there are a few specialized knots not included.

Cow-Tie Knot

Two knots that are very similar are the honda knot and the cow-tie knot, described here. The cow-tie knot has other names, but its primary use on the farm is for making a quick halter substitute from a rope, to tie up or tether an animal. Tie an overhand knot in the rope about six inches further from the end than the circumference of the animal's neck. Place the rope around the neck, pass the end through the overhand knot, tie another overhand knot in the end, then tighten up such that the resulting loop is just the size of the animal's neck.

Figure 80 - Cow-Tie Knot

Honda Knot

The honda knot is used to make a rope into a temporary lariat. It looks very similar to the cow-tie knot, but differs in two ways: it's used to make a much smaller loop and the end is not passed through the center of the overhand knot. This difference makes the loop align itself more closely with the standing part. A bowline could be used for the honda, but the honda knot is better; it leaves the center of the loop clear, where the bowline has an end that could restrict the loop's free running.

The honda knot was used by archers of Elizabethan time for the ends of their bowstrings. It is secure, but allows quick stringing and unstringing.

Figure 81 - Honda Knot

Halter Hitch

A common method to tie an animal to a rail or post is the halter hitch. It is simply a slipped overhand noose around the rail or post. It's quick to tie and a tug on the end releases it.

Figure 82 - Halter Hitch

Harness Loop

When you need to lash down a load, it's important to be able to tighten the lashing and hold it easily while securing the end. A good way is to form a loop in the lashing, pass the end around the securing point, then back through the loop, so that hauling on the end tightens the lashing. In the absence of friction, this would give a two to one mechanical advantage, but of course that's not how the world works – friction's always present. A common way to form the loop is to take a bight in the rope and tie an overhand knot in it. This is practical for the purpose – the problem comes when it's time to untie the jammed loop. A better way is the harness loop. Take two bights in the rope, pass one bight around the other, then draw the lower loop up through the top loop. Work the knot carefully into form. This knot is also useful when several people are hauling on the same rope. A harness loop for each keeps them spaced and gives them a good grip.

Figure 83 - Harness Loop

Butterfly Loop

Here's a knot that is used by farmers, climbers, linemen and anyone who needs a hauling loop or a means of connecting to the middle of a line. It's similar to the harness loop, but has a beautiful symmetry to it, as well as security. There are numerous ways to tie it, of which we show only two. Check the knot after forming it. It may take a bit of working to get it into its proper shape. If a strong pull on the ends has no effect on the loop size, it's probably good. This brings to mind a secondary use of the knot; if there's a bad or worn section, tie the knot so that the weak part forms the loop. It will be out of use and free from strain.

Start by taking a bight and giving it two half twists counterclockwise. (The direction of the twists determines whether you later pass the loop in front of, or behind, the center crossings.) Pass the resulting loop up behind the twists, between the standing parts and back down through the center of the twists. A simple way to do this is to put your right

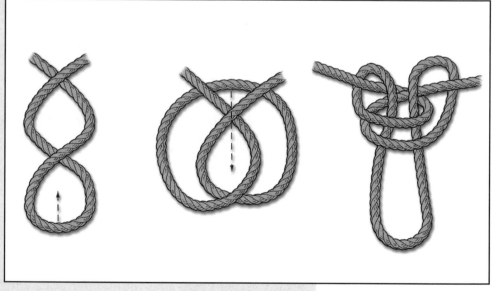

Figure 84 - Butterfly Loop

hand down through the loop formed by the twists, then up through the center twist. With your left hand grasp the loop that is around your right wrist, pull it down, then up between the standing parts and pass it to the right hand. With the right hand, pull it back through completely. The part you are holding forms the loop. Work the knot carefully into form, making the loop the size you need.

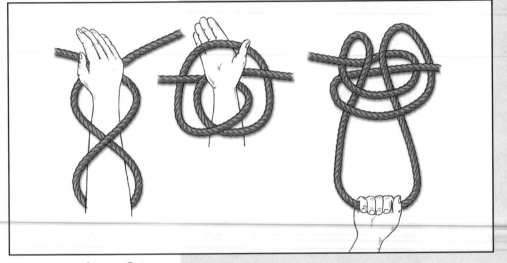

Figure 85 - Quick Butterfly Loop

Jug Sling and Emergency Bridle

In these days of steel vacuum bottles, the jug sling is an anachronism, but is included here for old time's sake. When a farmer took a mason jar or stone jug of water to the field, this was how he might have attached a cord to carry it. Be warned; it's not an easy knot to tie on the first try.

Cyrus Day, in *The Art of Knotting and Splicing*, describes seven ways to tie it, but here is the one Ashley recommends and it works. Start with a bight in the middle of the cord, folded back over the standing parts. Grip the bight and the parts it crosses with the left hand and, with the right, twist the two center parts a full turn. Then reach down through the center of that turn and grasp the original bight in the center and pull it up between the center parts. Pull the bight and the pair of ends apart to form the first stage of the sling. At this point there is one critical operation left. With your left hand, draw the bight marked with the arrow in step 3 back under the knot. The knot should now look symmetrical after some careful readjustment of parts. Slip it over the jar or jug (the neck goes where the X is on the illustration) and tighten. Tie the ends together in a reef or similar knot and the task is done.

It is said to be useful as an emergency bridle. The two center bights (A and B) go into the horse's mouth, the initial bight over the top of its head, the remainder of the knot around the muzzle, and the two ends become the reins. It would no doubt require a patient horse for installation.

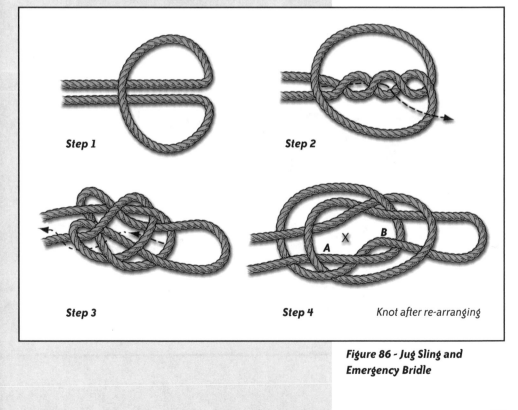

Step 1

Step 2

Step 3

Step 4   Knot after re-arranging

Figure 86 - Jug Sling and Emergency Bridle

Figure 87 - Farm Sling

Farm Sling

In days when hoisting bags of grain and bales of hay into the barn loft was a common task on the farm, this quick-release sling was a favourite. It can be applied with ease, it never jams and it is simple to make. It's just a foot-long piece of wood with a rope passing through it twice. The knot is optional, but Ashley's stopper would be a good choice.

Casting Cattle

This method of throwing a beef animal to the ground, given in old books of animal husbandry, has not been tested by this author, but is given here for interest's sake. Tie a bowline around the animal's neck, then a half hitch just behind the front legs, another just in front of the hind legs, being careful to avoid the udder in the case of a cow. If the rear half hitch is in front of the hip bone on one side, behind it on the other, it will be more likely to stay in position, not slipping too far forward or back. Hauling the rope to the rear should cast the animal, ready for the veterinary to take over.

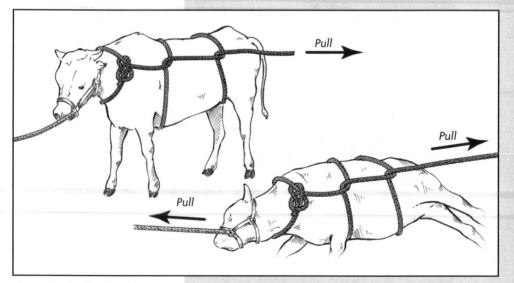

Figure 88 - Casting Cattle

Rope Ladder

Ladders made entirely of rope are difficult to climb and generally not worth the trouble to make. However, one made with rungs of wood or metal pipe can be quite handy and easily stored, even though it can't match a standard ladder for ease of use. The simplest knot to use for holding the rungs is the clove hitch. Be sure to include some means of preventing the rung from slipping out of the knot. A dowel through the rung on the outside end will do it, or drilling a hole there to hold a lashing of cord is even better.

Figure 89 - Rope Ladder

Lashings, Seizings and Frappings

When poles or ropes must be held together, a lashing or seizing is often the best choice, with frappings applied to hold them secure.

A device used in ships, mines and freight yards for hoisting and shifting heavy objects is called by the navy term 'sheers' or 'shear legs'. It consists of a pair of poles or spars with butts separated and secured, tops joined and sloping and held by guy lines. The hoisting tackle is hung from the junction. By easing or hauling the guy lines, the top may be raised or lowered with tremendous mechanical advantage. The pioneering farmer used the same principle for a device for pulling out stumps, roots and all. Sailors used a pair of spare spars to hoist water butts and swing them the short distance from shore to longboat when rewatering where docks did not exist.

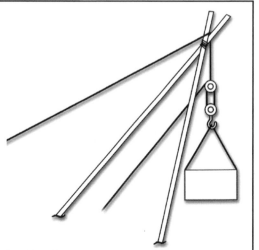

Figure 90 - Shear Legs

A common need when hoisting is to be done, is to make a tripod or bipod of poles or spars.

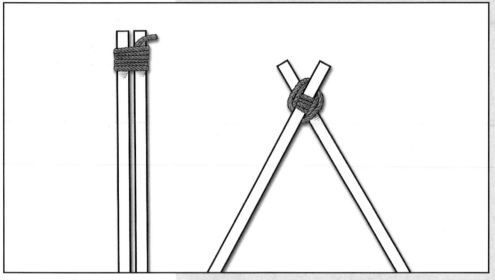

Figure 91 - Lashings

They can be lashed together with seizings, tightened by frapping. Whether a tripod or bipod is the intention, the method is the same. Form a clove hitch on one of the spars, wrap a number of turns around both, seizing them together, but not tightly, then spread the base ends to where you want them. Frapping then makes all tight and secure.

Figure 92 - Square Lashing

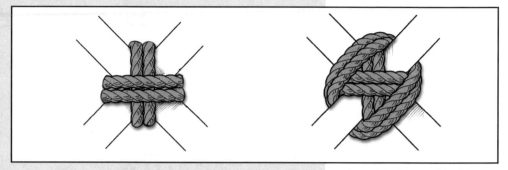

Figure 93 - Diagonal Lashing

If poles crossing at right angles are to be lashed together, as for a trellis or fence, a square lashing will hold them. If rigidity is important, adding diagonal struts will do it. They can be joined with a diagonal lashing.

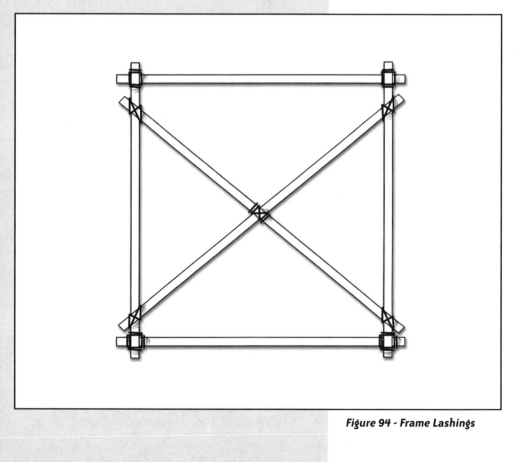

Figure 94 - Frame Lashings

Mechanical Advantage Using Rope

The usual means of gaining a mechanical advantage with rope is by use of the block and tackle. The mechanical advantage, not counting losses caused by friction, is equal to the number of ropes supporting the moving block.

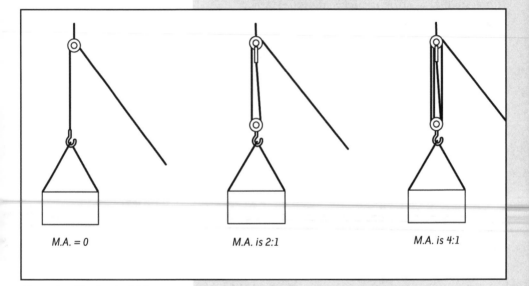

M.A. = 0   M.A. is 2:1   M.A. is 4:1

Figure 95 - Mechanical Advantage

There are ways of gaining mechanical advantage with rope when pulleys and winches aren't available.

Parbuckling

A method commonly used on the farm for loading a fuel drum into the back of a truck may be used to move any cylindrical object up a slope. The center of a rope is anchored behind the point to which the object is to be moved. The ends are then passed under the object and back up to the destination point. The operator hauling on the rope has a 2 to 1 mechanical advantage in rolling the object up the ramp. It's much better than trying to push a full drum of fuel up a ramp, losing control and having it bowl you over on its way down.

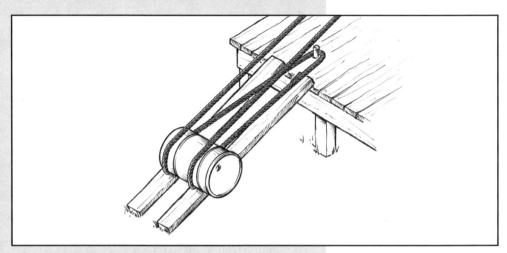

Figure 96 - Parbuckle

Spanish Windlass

The Spanish windlass is a sort of portable capstan, useful for moving a heavy object for a short distance. One end of the rope is attached to an anchor such as a tree, the other end to the object to be moved. A loop in the center of the rope is wrapped round an upright pole and a lever through the loop is used to wind the rope onto the pole, tightening the rope. It's easiest if there's one person controlling the pole while another works the lever.

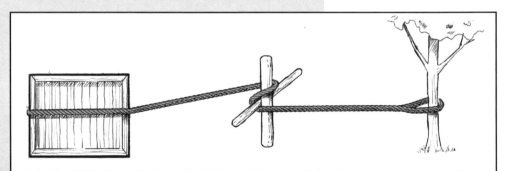

Figure 97 - Spanish Windlass

Heat-Treating the Ends

Heat-treating works well on rope material that melts. To avoid having the ends mushroom when you melt them, you can apply a short whipping (or a wrap of duct tape) and heat the rope all around just back of the whipping. Stretch the hot portion slightly to constrict it. Let it cool and harden, then cut the rope in the constricted zone.

If you'd rather avoid the extra time to whip it, heat the end, let it mushroom, and cool it. Then heat around the rope a short distance back from the end, stretch to constrict, cool and cut in the constriction.

If you don't mind dedicating a knife to the task, a neat system is to wrap tape round the section to be cut, then cut it with a red-hot knife, which seals as it cuts. A soldering gun with the flat, broad smoothing tip mounted does a creditable job. A somewhat more risky way is to heat the rope end to melt point, then wrap a heavy cloth around the end, draw the melted material out to a taper and let it harden.

Appendix 1
Fiber Characteristics

Manila

Manila rope is made from the strongest of the natural fibers. They come from the Philippine abaca plant, are normally around 5 feet long, but can be as long as 25 feet. Manila is the ideal natural rope material, dependable, with good resistance to sun, rain and wear, with little stretch.

Sisal

Sisal, from the Mexican and South American agave (sisalana) plant, is similar to manila, but rough, has shorter fibers and is not quite as strong. It has almost no stretch. It makes an economical general purpose rope. The natural texture of both sisal and manila means that they hold a knot well with little problem of slippage.

Other Natural Fibers

Hemp, made from the stem of several species of plants, was once an important twine, but is little used now as a fiber. Jute, though mostly used as sacking, was also used as the heart for wire ropes. Coir, from coconut husks, made a rather weak rope called a grass line, with poor resistance to wear and weather, but it floated, so had specific uses before being replaced by the poly fibers. Cotton and linen have little utility for ropes, but are used for whipping material.

Nylon

Nylon makes the strongest rope generally available. It stretches more than other fibers, which means that it can withstand the shock loading imposed on tow lines, anchor lines and starter cords. It won't rot if left wet and is highly resistant to wear and abrasion. It resists most acids, alkaline materials and organic solvents, but tropical sunlight can cause it to lose strength. It outlasts the natural fibers by a wide margin.

Polyester

Polyester rope is about twice as strong as manila and stretches more, but it's not nearly as stretchy as nylon and not quite as strong. Its resistance to abrasion, chemicals and weather is excellent.

Polypropylene

Polypropylene has one characteristic that sets it apart – it floats. Far stronger than manila, it remains flexible in cold weather, resists most acids and alkalis, stretches enough to have good resistance to shock loading and has long working life. For resistance to sunlight (UV), which can greatly reduce its strength, it is often stabilized with a pigment content, usually carbon black. It has extremely high electrical resistance, so is a favourite with electrical crews.

Other Synthetic Fibers

Some new fibers with many excellent qualities and a strength-to-weight ratio of five to ten times that of steel are available at somewhat higher cost. Examples are Dupont's Kevlar® and Allied Signal's Spectra®.

Appendix 2
Breaking Strength of Ropes of Various Fibers

Note: *The table below gives the approximate breaking strength in pounds for new three-strand twist rope. The strength of the various ropes can differ significantly. Always consult manufacturer's specifications for working strength.*

Diameter (inches)	Manila	Nylon	Polypropylene	Polyester	Sisal	Cotton
3/16	350	800	650	750	300	
1/4	600	1500	1200	1300	480	420
5/16	900	2300	1800	1980	800	665
3/8	1350	3500	2500	2900	1080	890
1/2	2650	6000	3900	5085	2120	1450
5/8	4400	9000	5800	7825	3520	
3/4	5400	13000	8000	11200	4320	
7/8	7700	18000	10500	15225	6160	
1	9000	23000	13000	19775	7200	
1-1/4	13500	35000	20000	29800	10800	
1-1/2	18500	50000	28000	42200	14800	
1-3/4	26500	74000	40000	54000	19000	
2	31000	87000	48000	72000	24800	
Wet Strength Factor	1.15	.85	1.0	1.0		1.15

Wet Strength Factor

The table above shows approximate breaking strength in pounds for dry rope. To calculate the breaking strength for wet rope, multiply by the wet strength factor.

Rule of Thumb

For a quick calculation of the strength of new manila rope, there's a rule of thumb that says the square of the rope diameter multiplied by 8000 gives the breaking strength. Its results are somewhat conservative. For example, for 1/2" rope, 1/2 x 1/2 x 8000 gives 2000 pounds breaking strength, below what suppliers usually claim.

Safety Factor

To calculate a safe working load for rope in good condition, divide the breaking strength by a safety factor of around 10 for rope under 1/2", 8 up to 3/4", 7 for larger sizes. For nylon, increase the factor by 2 (i.e., 12, 10 and 9).

Danger of Exceeding Working Strength of Rope

It's impossible to tell from surface inspection if a rope has been overstressed, causing internal fiber damage. The safe working load may be considerably less than the tabulated value of breaking strength. When a heavy load is supported overhead, the danger is obvious, but large rope of stretchy fibers such as nylon can be a serious source of danger to anyone in line with it or near it. When a nylon rope breaks under stress, it snaps back with speed and violence.

Appendix 3
Rope Care

1. Uncoiling new rope from a reel, or cord or fishing line from a spool, should be done by mounting the reel or spool on an axle and letting it turn as you draw the rope or line from it. This will avoid adding an unwanted twist. If the rope is in a coil, and you are uncoiling it from the center, it matters which side the coil is lying on when you begin. For regular lay (right-hand lay) the rope should uncoil in a counterclockwise direction. The added twist tends to tighten the lay, rather than to loosen it, which could cause hockling.

2. Natural fiber rope or cord should be dried thoroughly before storing.

3. Rust from iron or steel is highly damaging to rope, and dirt of any kind can act as an abrasive on the fibers. Keep rope clean; wash it if necessary and if it's a natural fiber, dry it carefully.

4. If rope is to be run on gear such as sheaves or pulleys, or through a thimble, be sure the gear is matched to the rope size to avoid sharp bending and abrasion. An old rule for power transmission in mines and factories by rope and pulley was to have a pulley diameter at least 50 times that of the rope, which is, of course, somewhat impractical for block and tackle.

5. Reverse ends of rope (or fly line) periodically so the wear will be even.

Appendix 4
Rope Fiber
Selection Summary

(In relative characteristics, numbers 1 to 5 indicate best to worst.)

Type of Fiber	Nylon	Polyester	Polypropylene	Polyethylene	Manila
Relative Strength	1	2	3	4	5
% Change in Strength when Wet	-15	0	0	0	+15
Shock Resistance Stretch % at Break Point	20 - 35	15 - 20	15 - 20	10 - 15	10 - 15
Specific Gravity	1.10 - 1.15 (Sinks)	1.38 (Sinks)	.90 (Floats)	.90 - .95 (Floats)	1.38 (Sinks)
UV Resistance	Good	Excellent	Poor	Fair	Good
Melting Point (°F)	414 - 460	450 - 500	300 - 330	275 - 300	Chars at 350
Relative Abrasion Resistance	2	1	4	5	3
Relative Flexing Damage Resistance	1	2	3	5	4

Appendix 5
Glossary

To talk about any subject, it's necessary to know the terminology. The following terms are used by those who work with lines. Some are used in the knot descriptions.

Abaca

A species of banana plant grown in the Philippines, the fiber of which is processed to become manila rope. The abaca is also grown in Central America, Sumatra and Borneo.

Acceleration stress

Additional stress placed on rope due to dynamic loading (see below), as when a load is dropped, lifted suddenly, or when a tow rope is tightened.

After-turn

In a rope the twist in the strands (generally left) is called "fore-turn", and the twist in the rope, always in the opposite direction to the strand twist, is called "after-turn".

Becket

A rope handle or an eye in a rope.

Bend

A knot used to join two ropes or cords.

Bight

Similar to a loop, and sometimes so called. To a sailor, a bight was closed no more tightly than a semicircle. A bay could be called a bight, which meant it was sufficiently open for a ship to sail out of it on a single tack.

Bitt(s)

A post or pair of posts with or without a crossbar for securing heavy lines, usually in the bow of a boat or on a dock.

Bitter end

The end of a cable or hawser at the bitt (or bollard) on the deck of a ship. When the anchor cable had been paid out to the bitter end, no more was available, which some students of English believe is the source of the expression, "holding out until the bitter end", that is, as long as possible.

Blend

A combination rope or mix of different synthetic fibers to form one rope. Many such exist for special purposes. Breaking strength specifications for such ropes should be obtained from the manufacturer, as general specifications are not reliable.

Block

A system of pulleys mounted in a case, of which there are many kinds – single, double, snatch, cheek, etc. The rope runs over the sheave (pulley) set between the two shells (cheeks) of the block.

Brown filament

Monofilament polypropylene into which is blown a gas during extrusion to produce a lighter, less expensive and less strong rope, but one that will float.

Bollard

A heavy post for securing lines; it may be on a ship or on a dock.

Braid

A type of rope produced by braiding the yarns rather than twisting them.

Breaking strength

The tensile strength, or the measured load required to break a rope in tension. The testing method conforms to precise requirements, which usually include new rope, eye-spliced, with tension applied at a controlled rate.

Coefficient of friction

The effective ability of a rope to grip or be gripped. It is important where a slippery rope can be dangerous or cause difficulty in its use.

Combination cordage

A blend of two or more materials into one cord. May have an outer sleeve of polyester with a light weight core of polypropylene.

Cordage

General term for line, twisted or braided; usually refers to sizes of one inch diameter and under.

Creep

The "taffy effect"; a slow flow of a synthetic material such as polypropylene under high temperature or stress.

Crown splice

Splicing the end of a rope into itself to prevent fraying and unravelling as an alternative to whipping.

Dacron®

Dupont de Nemours Co. trade name for polyester.

Diamond braid

Cordage construction with 8, 12 or 16 strands of fibers braided under and over each other in a circular direction. The center of the rope may be hollow, such as in hollow braid, allowing for easy splicing, or it may have a center core of parallel fibers.

Dielectric

A non-conductor of electricity. Polypropylene rope has excellent dielectric properties.

Double braid

Cordage construction with a jacket braided over a braided rope core. It is like two ropes in one. Strong and flexible, it doesn't hockle, kink or rotate under a load, and is spliceable; it's also called braid on braid, double spliceable braid and yacht braid.

Dynamic loading

A sudden force applied to a rope; for example, picking up a tow on a slack line or stopping a falling object.

End

The end of the rope, the part with which you'll usually be working.

Eye

A spliced, seized or knotted loop.

Eye splice

A fixed loop formed in the end of a line by splicing the end back into its standing part.

Fathom

A nautical unit of measurement; a fathom is six feet.

Fiber

A natural or synthetic filament capable of being spun into yarn.

Fid

A tapering pin used to open the strands of a rope for splicing. It is sometimes hollow, usually made of wood and, though similar to a marlinespike, is usually larger.

Four stage construction

A manufacturing process for making three-strand twisted rope:
  (1) twisting fibers into one-ply yarn;
  (2) twisting these yarns into three-ply yarn;
  (3) forming the strand;
  (4) twisting three strands together into finished rope.

Frapping

When a lashing is applied to spars, ropes or cables, the frapping turns are applied perpendicular to the main lashing to tighten it and add security.

Guy lines

Lines used to steady, guide or support something such as a mast or load.

Halyard

Line used to hoist or lower a sail or a flag.

Hand

The feel of rope to the touch, its roughness, slipperiness, flexibility, etc.

Hawser

A line used in mooring, anchoring or towing vessels.

Hemp

The fibers of *Cannabis sativa*. Sometimes refers to a fiber similar to true hemp such as manila.

Henequin

The *Agave fourcroydes*, a plant of Yucatan, used in making sisal.

Hitch

A knot used to secure a line to an object.

Hockle

A twist against the lay, taking twist out of a rope. It reduces tensile strength. An advantage of braided rope is that it doesn't hockle. (More recently, hockle has come to include the kinking of a braided rope from yarns popping out of the cover.)

Hollow braid

Braided rope or cord without a central core; more readily spliced than solid core rope.

Jute

A natural fiber obtained from either of two Asian plants, *Corchorus capsulans* or *Corchorus olitorius*; used in sacking, twine and cordage.

Kink

A sharp bend or twist in a rope that permanently distorts the strands.

Lariat

A specially constructed rope with a running noose for catching livestock; also called a lasso.

Lashing

Binding or seizing; most often used to hold a pair of spars, ropes or cables together.

Lay

The direction of twist of the parts of a rope or cable. A right-hand lay is such that the strands have the same orientation as the threads of a right-hand screw. Commonly the main strands of a rope are laid to the right (Z twist), but the yarns in each individual strand are left-laid (S twist). May be expressed as hard, regular or soft lay.

Left hand twist

An S-twist or a twist that would be unlaid in a counterclockwise direction.

Life line

An anchored line used as a support to someone who may fall or drown; a line rigged to keep the crew from being washed overboard in bad weather.

Line

A cable, hawser, rope, string, cord or wire.

Long splice

A way to join two pieces of a stranded rope without increasing its diameter. The short splice is stronger but thickens the rope, preventing its use in a pulley where rope diameter may not be increased.

Manila

A fiber of the abaca plant used in making rope.

Marlinespike

(Also marlinspike.) A pointed iron spike used to separate strands of rope when splicing.

Mooring line

A rope or cable used to make fast a boat or aircraft to a dock.

Natural fiber

A plant fiber such as cotton, jute, manila, sisal or hemp.

Nylon

Any of a family of high strength, resilient synthetic materials.

Olefin

A class of unsaturated hydrocarbons. Polypropylene and polyethylene are both made of olefin fibers.

Overhand loop

A loop with the end crossed over the standing part.

Ply

One of the strands twisted together to make yarn, rope, thread or twine; used in combination to indicate a specified number of strands (example: two ply).

Polyester

A synthetic fiber used for its strength and resistance to ultraviolet deterioration.

Polypropylene

A strong synthetic fiber material, waterproof, resistant to rot, and light enough to float in water.

Right hand twist

A Z-twist, a twist that would be unlaid in a clockwise direction.

Rope

Cordage, usually of 1/4" diameter or greater. It may be twisted or braided, of natural or synthetic fibers or wire.

Safety factor

A number that the tensile (breaking) strength is divided by, in order to determine the safe working load. It applies to new rope in good condition with proper splices.

Seizing

A lashing of smaller cordage generally used to wrap, whip or otherwise confine one or more ropes, spars or cables with smaller material; among its uses are to prevent fraying or unlaying, and to keep a knot from spilling.

Sheave

A grooved wheel or roller in a block or pulley over which the rope passes.

Short splice

A method for joining rope end to end, used when maximum strength is required; causes increase in diameter.

Sisal

The fiber of the *Agave sisalana*, or *Agave fourcroydes*, used for making cordage and rope.

Sling

A rope or system of ropes used for hoisting.

Slippery

A term applied to a knot that may be spilled by yanking an end.

Solid braid

A construction of 9, 12, or 18 strands of fiber, lock-stitched together. It works well with pulleys and winches, as it is smooth, round and firm, holding its shape well under pressure and load; however, it is not as strong as other braids, nor is it spliceable.

Spar

A mast, yard, pole or boom.

Splice

To join ropes by inter-weaving strands or braids.

Standing part

The rest of the rope, away from the end.

Strand

Two or more yarns twisted together; strands twisted or plaited together form a rope.

S-twist

Left hand twist, a twist that would be unlaid by turning the yarn or rope in a counterclockwise direction.

Synthetic fiber

A non-organic fiber, produced by chemical means.

Tackle

A means of gaining mechanical advantage by a line run through two or more blocks; the mechanical advantage is determined by the number of lines supporting the load. (Also called block and tackle).

Tensile strength

The resistance of rope to a force tending to break it; also called the breaking strength, or the force that must be applied to break a rope.

Thimble

A metal insert, either round or somewhat pear-shaped, spliced into the end of a rope for taking a hook or shackle. The line fits into the concave outside; the convex inside bears the strain and wear.

Underhand loop

A loop with the end crossed under the standing part.

UV resistance

Ability of a rope fiber to withstand decay from the damaging effect of the ultraviolet rays of the sun.

Whipping

The binding of the end of a rope with several turns of cord to prevent unlaying; the cord or thread used to do so.

Working load

The weight recommended for safe working conditions, for new rope in good condition with appropriate splices and normal service conditions. (Also called working strength.)

Yarn

Textile fibers twisted together form yarns. Yarns twisted together form strands.

Z-twist

Right handed twist; a twist that would be unlaid by turning the yarn or rope in a clockwise direction.

Appendix 6
Some Books on Knots

There are plenty of knot books out there, some good, some not so good. This list represents some of the better ones.

Ashley, Clifford W.,
The Ashley Book of Knots,
Doubleday and Co., New York.
This is the classic knot book, respected as the best source of ropework knowledge in existence. It's sometimes hard to find, as it goes out of print periodically, and used copies are snapped up immediately.

Day, Cyrus L.,
The Art of Knotting and Splicing,
Naval Institute Press, Annapolis, Maryland.
Another classic, Day's book has appeared in several editions. Its one drawback, which some might consider an advantage, is that its illustrations are photographs rather than drawings, so they lack the clarity a drawing can achieve. He has also produced a smaller volume, suitable for hip-pocket transportation.

Budworth, Geoffrey,
The Complete Book of Decorative Knots,
Hamlyn, London.
As the title indicates, Budworth's book is for those interested in decorative knots, the Turk's head, for example, the many versions of which we do not cover in this volume.

Merry, Barbara,
The Splicing Handbook,
International Marine Publishing Company, Camden, Maine.
Another specialty item, Merry's book has little to say about the standard knots, but gives well-illustrated advice on splicing techniques for both modern and traditional ropes, including rope-to-chain and rope-to-wire joins.

Jarman, Colin, and Beavis, Bill,
Modern Rope Seamanship,
International Marine Publishing Company,
Camden, Maine.
This is very good for coverage of the use of the
various knots aboard ship, including elements of
seamanship, decorative ropework and splicing of
laid, braided and wire ropes.

Smith, Hervey Garrett,
The Marlinspike Sailor,
International Marine Publishing Company,
Camden, Maine.
For all the fancy jobs aboard ship, such as plaiting
a bell lanyard, making a nice-looking fender or
stropping a block.

Black, Joe,
Horses, Hitches and Rocky Trails,
Swallow Press, 1959.
An old-timer's advice on loading and handling a
string of pack horses, with a masterful exposition
of the diamond hitch.

Index